Illinois Learning Standards

STATE GOAL 14: Understand political systems, with an emphasis on the United States.

14.A.2 Explain the importance of fundamental concepts expressed and implied in major documents including the Declaration of Independence, the United States Constitution and the Illinois Constitution.

14.B.2 Explain what government does at local, state and national levels.

14.C.2 Describe and evaluate why rights and responsibilities are important to the individual, family, community, workplace, state and nation (e. g., voting, protection under the law).

14.D.2 Explain ways that individuals and groups influence and shape public policy.

14.E.2 Determine and explain the leadership role of the United States in international settings.

14.F.2 Identify consistencies and inconsistencies between expressed United States political traditions and ideas and actual practices (e.g., freedom of speech, right to bear arms, slavery, voting rights).

STATE GOAL 15: Understand economic systems, with an emphasis on the United States.

15.A.2a Explain how economic systems decide what goods and services are produced, how they are produced and who consumes them.

15.A.2b Describe how incomes reflect choices made about education and careers.

15.A.2c Describe unemployment.

15.B.2a Identify factors that affect how consumers make their choices.

15.B.2b Explain the relationship between the quantity of goods/services purchased and their price.

15.B.2c Explain that when a choice is made, something else is given up.

15.C.2a Describe the relationship between price and quantity supplied of a good or service.

15.C.2b Identify and explain examples of competition in the economy.

15.C.2c Describe how entrepreneurs take risks in order to produce goods or services.

15.D.2a Explain why people and countries voluntarily exchange goods and services.

15.D.2b Describe the relationships among specialization, division of labor, productivity of workers and interdependence among producers and consumers.

15E.2a Explain how and why public goods and services are provided.

15.E.2b Identify which public goods and services are provided by differing levels of government.

STATE GOAL 16: Understand events, trends, individuals and movements shaping the history of Illinois, the United States and other nations.

16.A.2a Read historical stories and determine events which influenced their writing.

16.A.2b Compare different stories about a historical figure or event and analyze differences in the portrayals and perspectives they present.

16.A.2c Ask questions and seek answers by collecting and analyzing data from historic documents, images and other literary and non-literary sources.

16.B.2a (US) Describe how the European colonies in North America developed politically.

16.B.2b (US) Identify major causes of the American Revolution and describe the consequences of the Revolution through the early national period, including the roles of George Washington, Thomas Jefferson and Benjamin Franklin.

16.B.2c (US) Identify presidential elections that were pivotal in the formation of modern political parties.

16.B.2d (US) Identify major political events and leaders within the United States historical eras since the adoption of the Constitution, including the westward expansion, Louisiana Purchase, Civil War, and 20th century wars as well as the roles of Thomas Jefferson, Abraham Lincoln, Woodrow Wilson, and Franklin D. Roosevelt.

16.B.2a (W) Describe the historical development of monarchies, oligarchies and city-states in ancient civilizations.

16.B.2b (W) Describe the origins of Western political ideas and institutions (e.g. Greek democracy, Roman republic, Magna Carta and Common Law, the Enlightenment).

16.C.2a (US) Describe how slavery and indentured servitude influenced the early economy of the United States.

16.C.2b (US) Explain how individuals, including John Deere, Thomas Edison, Robert McCormack, George Washington Carver and Henry Ford, contributed to economic change through ideas, inventions and entrepreneurship.

16.C.2c (US) Describe significant economic events including industrialization, immigration, the Great Depression, the shift to a service economy and the rise of technology that influenced history from the industrial development era to the present.

16.C.2a (W) Describe the economic consequences of the first agricultural revolution, 4000 BCE-1000 BCE.

16.C.2b (W) Describe the basic economic systems of the world's great civilizations including Mesopotamia, Egypt, Aegean/Mediterranean and Asian civilizations, 1000 BCE - 500 CE.

16.C.2c (W) Describe basic economic changes that led to and resulted from the manorial agricultural system, the industrial revolution, the rise of the capitalism and the information/communication revolution.

16.D.2a (US) Describe the various individual motives for settling in colonial America.

16.D.2b (US) Describe the ways in which participation in the westward movement affected families and communities.

16.D.2c US) Describe the influence of key individuals and groups, including Susan B. Anthony/suffrage and Martin Luther King, Jr./civil rights, in the historical eras of Illinois and the United States.

16.D.2 (W) Describe the various roles of men, women and children in the family, at work, and in the community in various time periods and places (e.g., ancient Rome, Medieval Europe, ancient China, Sub-Saharan Africa).

16.E.2a (US) Identify environmental factors that drew settlers to the state and region.

16.E.2b US) Identify individuals and events in the development of the conservation movement including John Muir, Theodore Roosevelt and the creation of the National Park System.

16.E.2c (US) Describe environmental factors that influenced the development of transportation and trade in Illinois.

16.E.2a (W) Describe how people in hunting and gathering and early pastoral societies adapted to their respective environments.

16.E.2b (W) Identify individuals and their inventions (e.g., Watt/ steam engine, Nobel/TNT, Edison/electric light) which influenced world environmental history.

STATE GOAL 17: Understand world geography and the effects of geography on society, with an emphasis on the United States.

17.A.2a Compare the physical characteristics of places including soils, land forms, vegetation, wildlife, climate, natural hazards.

17.A.2b Use maps and other geographic representations and instruments to gather information about people, places and environments.

17.B.2a Describe how physical and human processes shape spatial patterns including erosion, agriculture and settlement.

17.B.2b Explain how physical and living components interact in a variety of ecosystems including desert, prairie, flood plain, forest, tundra.

17.C.2a Describe how natural events in the physical environment affect human activities.

17.C.2b Describe the relationships among location of resources, population distribution and economic activities (e.g., transportation, trade, communications).

17.C.2c Explain how human activity affects the environment.

17.D.2a Describe how physical characteristics of places influence people's perceptions and their roles in the world over time.

17.D.2b Identify different settlement patterns in Illinois and the United States and relate them to physical features and resources.

STATE GOAL 18: Understand social systems, with an emphasis on the United States.

18.A.2 Explain ways in which language, stories, folk tales, music, media and artistic creations serve as expressions of culture.

18.B.2a Describe interactions of individuals, groups and institutions in situations drawn from the local community (e.g., local response to state and national reforms).

18.B.2b Describe the ways in which institutions meet the needs of society.

18.C.2 Describe how changes in production (e.g., hunting and gathering, agricultural, industrial) and population caused changes in social systems.

ILLINOIS
Macmillan/McGraw-Hill **TIMELINKS**

The United States

PROGRAM AUTHORS

James A. Banks
Kevin P. Colleary
Linda Greenow
Walter C. Parker
Emily M. Schell
Dinah Zike

CONTRIBUTORS

Raymond C. Jones
Irma M. Olmedo

 Macmillan/McGraw-Hill

Volume I

PROGRAM AUTHORS

James A. Banks, Ph.D.
Kerry and Linda Killinger
    Professor of Diversity Studies
    and Director, Center for
    Multicultural Education
University of Washington
Seattle, Washington

Kevin P. Colleary, Ed.D.
Curriculum and Teaching Department
Graduate School of Education
Fordham University
New York, New York

Linda Greenow, Ph.D.
Associate Professor and Chair
Department of Geography
State University of New York at
    New Paltz
New Paltz, New York

Walter C. Parker, Ph.D.
Professor of Social Studies Education,
University of Washington
Seattle, Washington

Emily M. Schell, Ed.D.
Visiting Professor, Teacher Education
San Diego State University
San Diego, California

Dinah Zike
Educational Consultant
Dinah-Mite Activities, Inc.
San Antonio, Texas

CONTRIBUTORS

Raymond C. Jones, Ph.D.
Director of Secondary Social Studies
    Education
Wake Forest University
Winston-Salem, North Carolina

Irma M. Olmedo
Associate Professor
University of Illinois-Chicago
College of Education
Chicago, Illinois

HISTORIANS/SCHOLARS

Rabbi Pamela Barmash, Ph.D.
Associate Professor of Hebrew Bible
    and Biblical Hebrew and Director,
    Program in Jewish, Islamic and Near
    Eastern Studies
Washington University
St. Louis, Missouri

Thomas Bender, Ph.D.
Professor of History
New York University
New York, New York

Ned Blackhawk
Associate Professor of History and
    American Indian Studies
University of Wisconsin
Madison, Wisconsin

Chun-shu Chang
Professor of History
University of Michigan
Ann Arbor, Michigan

Manuel Chavez, Ph.D.
Associate Director, Center for Latin
    American & Caribbean Studies,
    Assistant Professor, School of
    Journalism
Michigan State University
East Lansing, Michigan

Sheilah F. Clarke-Ekong, Ph.D.
Professor of Anthropology
University of Missouri-St. Louis
St. Louis, Missouri

Lawrence Dale, Ph.D.
Director, Center for Economic
    Education
Arkansas State University
Jonesboro, Arkansas

Mac Dixon-Fyle, Ph.D.
Professor of History
DePauw University
Greencastle, Indiana

Carl W. Ernst
William R. Kenan, Jr., Distinguished
    Professor
Department of Religious Studies
Director, Carolina Center for the
    Study of the Middle East and Muslim
    Civilizations
University of North Carolina
Chapel Hill, North Carolina

Brooks Green, Ph.D.
Associate Professor of Geography
University of Central Arkansas
Conway, Arkansas

Sumit Guha, Ph.D.
Professor of History
Rutgers
The State University of New Jersey
New Brunswick, New Jersey

Thomas C. Holt, Ph.D.
Professor of History
University of Chicago
Chicago, Illinois

Richard E. Keady, Ph.D.
Professor, Comparative Religious
    Studies
San Jose State University
San Jose, California

The **McGraw-Hill** Companies

Macmillan
McGraw-Hill

The United States
CONTENTS, Volume 1

Why do people take risks?

Reference Section

Skills and Features

Maps

Introduction To . . .

Introduction

EXPLORE The Big Idea

Essential Question
What do places, people, and ideas tell us about the United States?

FOLDABLES Study Organizer

Organizing Information
Make and label a Concept Map Foldable before you read the overview. Write the words **United States** at the top. Label the three tabs **Places**, **People**, and **Ideas**. Use the Foldable to organize information.

United States
Places | People | Ideas

LOG ON

For more information go to
www.macmillanmh.com

1

Our Nation's Geography

Illinois Learning Standards
17.A.2a, 17.A.2b, 17.B.2b, 17.C.2a

WHERE IS OUR NATION?

The main area of the United States stretches from Canada to Mexico and from the Atlantic Ocean to the Pacific Ocean. Forty-eight states are located in that area. Alaska is located at the northwest edge of North America. Hawaii is a chain of islands in the Pacific Ocean. Within this enormous area, many different landforms can be seen.

Plateaus and Basins

A plateau is a flat landform that rises above surrounding land. The largest plateau in the United States is the Colorado Plateau in Utah, Arizona, New Mexico, and Colorado. A basin lies below the surrounding land. The Great Basin covers about 190,000 square miles in Nevada, Utah, Arizona, New Mexico, and Texas.

The Badlands of North Dakota

Redwood trees in California

Rivers and Lakes

For many years, rivers were the main highways for transporting people and goods across the United States. The Mississippi River in the longest river in the United States. Lakes are also part of our nation's geography. The Great Salt Lake lies in northern Utah and is the largest saltwater lake in the Western Hemisphere. The freshwater Great Lakes form part of our northern border with Canada. The Great Lakes are Huron, Ontario, Michigan, Erie, and Superior.

Environment and Ecosystems

The **environment** is everything that surrounds us. Natural resources are an important part of the environment. Natural resources include minerals such as copper, gold, and iron. Other natural resources include fossil fuels such as natural gas, coal, and oil. These are called nonrenewable resources because they cannot be replaced when they are taken from Earth. Trees, fish, and animals are also natural resources. These resources can be replaced, so they are called renewable resources. Trees, for example, can be replaced when they are cut down by planting new trees.

An **ecosystem** is a single environment that includes all living and nonliving things in a certain area. The United States has six kinds of ecosystems:

- croplands
- forests
- coasts and oceans
- urban and suburban areas
- arid and range areas
- freshwater areas

QUICK CHECK

Compare and Contrast **What is the difference between an environment and an ecosystem?**

▼ **Grand Teton National Park, Wyoming**

Sleeping Bear Dunes on Lake Michigan

The Five Regions

The United States can be divided into five geographic regions. A **region** is a large area with features, such as landforms and climate, that set it apart from other areas. The five regions of the United States are the Northeast, the Southeast, the Midwest, the Southwest, and the West.

Weather Patterns

Climate is weather over a number of years. The weather of a place includes its wind pattern, temperature, and the amount of precipitation, or rain or snow, that falls. If you divide the United States roughly in half from north to south, the eastern part is humid, or wet. The humid half gets more than 20 inches of precipitation each year. In contrast, the western half is arid, or dry. Arid areas get less than 20 inches of precipitation each year.

QUICK CHECK

Cause and Effect How do natural forces such as hurricanes affect certain regions?

WA
AK
OR
ID
NV
West
CA
UT
HI
AZ

Midwest

The Midwest is a region of plains and prairies. The Mississippi River begins in the Midwest, in northern Minnesota. The Midwest has extreme weather conditions. From spring through autumn, thunderstorms and tornadoes are a constant danger.

West

The West region includes eleven states. Two states, Alaska and Hawaii, do not have borders on the rest of the United States. Natural forces shape the region. In 2000 fires caused by lightning destroyed about 7 million acres of forest. The Rocky Mountains run north and south through the West region.

Southwest

The Southwest includes four states: Arizona, New Mexico, Texas, and Oklahoma. One of the best-known landforms in the United States, the Grand Canyon, is in the Southwest. Natural forces changed this region as well. The force of water over hundreds of millions of years changed a plateau into the ecosystem we call the Grand Canyon.

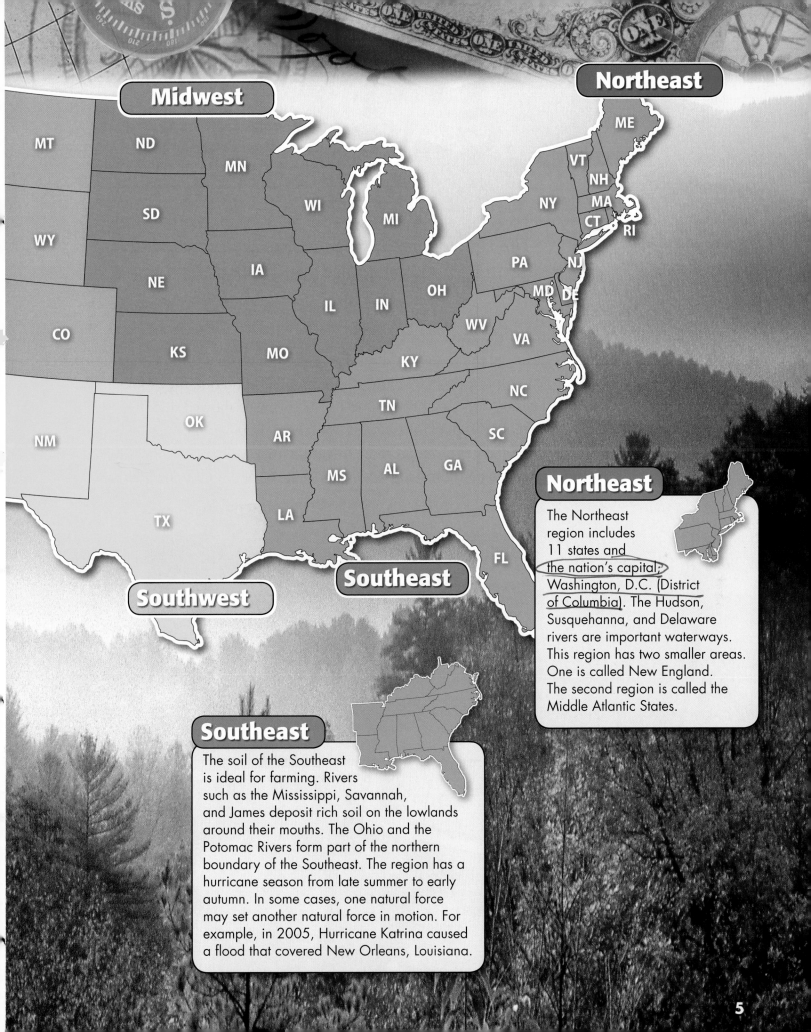

Midwest

Northeast

			ME
MT	ND		VT
	MN		NH
SD	WI	MI	NY	MA
WY	IA		CT	RI
NE	IL	IN	OH	PA	NJ
CO			WV	MD	DE
KS	MO	KY	VA
		TN	NC
NM	OK	AR		SC
		MS	AL	GA
TX	LA		FL

Southwest

Southeast

Northeast

The Northeast region includes 11 states and the nation's capital, Washington, D.C. (District of Columbia). The Hudson, Susquehanna, and Delaware rivers are important waterways. This region has two smaller areas. One is called New England. The second region is called the Middle Atlantic States.

Southeast

The soil of the Southeast is ideal for farming. Rivers such as the Mississippi, Savannah, and James deposit rich soil on the lowlands around their mouths. The Ohio and the Potomac Rivers form part of the northern boundary of the Southeast. The region has a hurricane season from late summer to early autumn. In some cases, one natural force may set another natural force in motion. For example, in 2005, Hurricane Katrina caused a flood that covered New Orleans, Louisiana.

People and Government

A DIVERSE PEOPLE

The United States is much more than a geographic location or collection of regions. The United States is also a nation of people and laws.

Counting the Population

In 1790 the founders of the United States wanted to know how many Americans lived in the new nation. To find out, they took a **census,** or population count. The first census showed that the population of the United States was about 3,900,000 people. More than 90 percent lived in rural, or country, areas. In 2006 the United States had an estimated population of about 300 million people.

A Christian Church

A Jewish synagogue

About 79 percent of people live in urban, or city, areas. The nation has changed!

The United States is sometimes called a nation of **immigrants**. Immigrants are people who leave one country to live in another country. Except for Native Americans, most Americans have someone in their family history who was an immigrant. This includes African Americans whose ancestors were enslaved and brought to North and South America against their will.

Immigration Continues

The first Europeans to come to America were English, Dutch, Swedish, Spanish, and French. Then, between 1870 and 1924, most of the immigrants entering the United States were from Southern and Eastern European countries such as Italy and Russia. Since 1965, many Asians—people from China, Korea, Vietnam, the Philippines, and other countries—have entered the United States.

Since 2000 many people from Latin America—Mexico, Central America, the West Indies, and South America—have come to the United States. Today, the United States has citizens from almost every ethnic group. An **ethnic group** is made up of people who share the same customs, language, and history.

America's Many Beliefs

Some early immigrants to North America came for religious reasons. From its earliest days, the United States allowed people to practice their religions without interference. The United States has never had an official church or religion. In fact, the first amendment, or addition, to the United States Constitution protects the freedom of religion.

QUICK CHECK

Making Inferences Why is the United States sometimes called a "nation of immigrants"?

A Hindu Temple

A Muslim Mosque

OUR GOVERNMENT

Two words that are often used to describe the United States are democracy and republic. In a democracy, power is held by the people. They use that power when they vote. A republic is a country with elected leaders who represent the people. The United States is known as a democratic republic.

The Constitution

In 1787 Americans met to create a government for the new nation. They wrote a constitution, or plan of government, for the new United States. The United States Constitution begins with a long sentence that is called the Preamble. It begins with the words, "We the people of the United States . . ." This means that the American people are not "ruled" by their leaders. Instead, government comes from the people. Everyone, including people in positions of power, must obey the Constitution. This is known as the rule of law.

The Constitution also gives Americans certain rights. The rights are included in a section known as the Bill of Rights. You will read more about the Constitution and the Bill of Rights in Unit 5.

▼ Celebration at the Capitol Building, Washington, D.C.

A student campaigns for class president

Types of Government

In the United States, there are three levels of government: local, state, and national. Local and state governments provide for the needs of the people in towns, cities, counties, and an entire state. The national, or federal, government serves the whole country.

Just as governments at all levels have a responsibility to serve the people, people have responsibilities as **citizens**. A citizen is someone who is born in a country or who becomes a member of that country by law. Some of the most important responsibilities of a citizen are listed on this page.

Citizens' Responsibilities

- Good citizens vote.
- Good citizens learn about political candidates and important issues.
- Good citizens obey local, state, and federal laws.
- Good citizens serve as jurors.
- Good citizens treat all people equally.
- Good citizens support government by paying taxes.

QUICK CHECK

Making Inferences Why is the United States called a democratic republic?

A citizen casts a vote in a voting booth

The American Economy

FARMING TO TECHNOLOGY

Illinois Learning Standards
15.A.2a, 15.B.2a, 15.B.2b, 15.B.2c, 15.C.2a, 15.E.2a, 15.E.2b

*Today, the United States has the largest **economy** in the world. An economy is the way a country uses its natural resources, money, and knowledge to produce goods and services.*

A Changing Economy

The early American economy depended on farming. Later, manufacturing made up the largest part of the economy. Today, the fastest-growing parts of the economy are finance and technology. The finance industry includes banks, credit card companies, and the stock market. The technology industry produces many kinds of products, from artificial body parts to airplane controls.

A Free Market

The gross domestic product (GDP) of our nation is the highest in the world. The GDP is the total amount of goods produced in the nation in one year. One reason for America's strong economy is that the United States has a free market economy. People have choices about how they earn and spend money. Store owners can decide what kind of stores to open. Factory owners can decide what products to make and what price to charge. A street vendor decides what items to sell, where to sell them, and what price to charge.

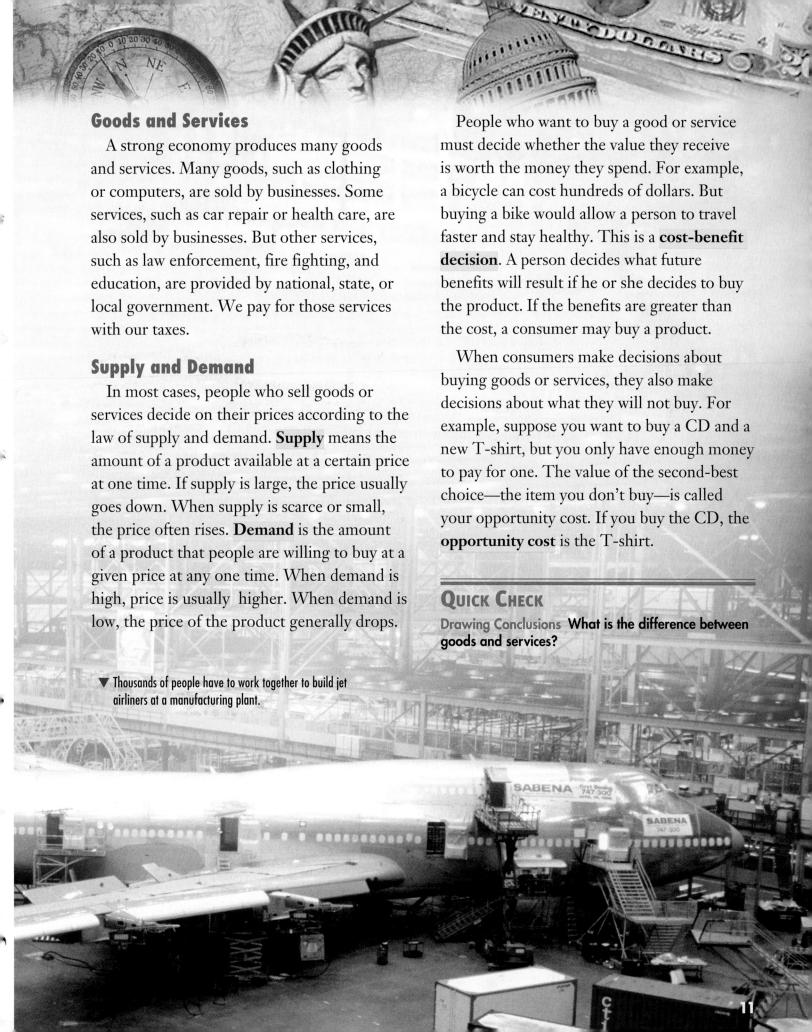

Goods and Services

A strong economy produces many goods and services. Many goods, such as clothing or computers, are sold by businesses. Some services, such as car repair or health care, are also sold by businesses. But other services, such as law enforcement, fire fighting, and education, are provided by national, state, or local government. We pay for those services with our taxes.

Supply and Demand

In most cases, people who sell goods or services decide on their prices according to the law of supply and demand. **Supply** means the amount of a product available at a certain price at one time. If supply is large, the price usually goes down. When supply is scarce or small, the price often rises. **Demand** is the amount of a product that people are willing to buy at a given price at any one time. When demand is high, price is usually higher. When demand is low, the price of the product generally drops.

▼ Thousands of people have to work together to build jet airliners at a manufacturing plant.

People who want to buy a good or service must decide whether the value they receive is worth the money they spend. For example, a bicycle can cost hundreds of dollars. But buying a bike would allow a person to travel faster and stay healthy. This is a **cost-benefit decision**. A person decides what future benefits will result if he or she decides to buy the product. If the benefits are greater than the cost, a consumer may buy a product.

When consumers make decisions about buying goods or services, they also make decisions about what they will not buy. For example, suppose you want to buy a CD and a new T-shirt, but you only have enough money to pay for one. The value of the second-best choice—the item you don't buy—is called your opportunity cost. If you buy the CD, the **opportunity cost** is the T-shirt.

QUICK CHECK

Drawing Conclusions **What is the difference between goods and services?**

History and Culture

PAST TO PRESENT

VOCABULARY

historian p. 12

artifacts p. 12

culture p. 12

primary source p. 13

secondary source p. 13

Illinois Learning Standards
16.A.2c, 18.A.2

*We study history to learn about the past.
What happened in the past often helps us understand
what is happening today.*

Clues from the Past

Historians, people who study the past, examine clues and records from people who lived long ago. These clues tell them what caused certain events. Historians also study human-made objects, called **artifacts**. Artifacts include pottery, clothing, and tools. These artifacts tell historians a great deal about the **culture**—beliefs, customs, and daily life—of people in the past.

Sources of the Past

Some historians study oral history. This is information that is told rather than written down. You may have oral history stories in your own family. It is how you learned what your parents or grandparents did when they were children. It is part of your culture.

Historians also use **primary sources** and **secondary sources** to understand why people acted in certain ways. A primary source is information that comes directly from a time period being studied. It could be letters, diaries, official documents, or photographs. A secondary source is material written by a person who did not witness the event being studied.

History Around Us

Many people think we learn about history only by reading books or visiting museums. But history is all around us. Some towns and cities have historic areas. Among them are the colonial buildings of Beacon Hill in Boston, Massachusetts, and the old Spanish missions in California—all built in the 1700s. Historic sites, such as presidential homes or battlefields, are also national historical monuments. Even if your town is new and has no historic sites, you are still surrounded by history. Was your town farmland or forest? What were the main roads? Which Native Americans lived there?

You have a part in history, too. You can learn about the history of your own family by asking older relatives about their memories of the past. Their scrapbooks, photos, newspaper clippings, and letters can teach you about your family's history. Someday historians may study the way you lived to learn about life in the early twenty-first century!

▲ Family albums are history too.

◀ Civil War reenactors talk to school children.

QUICK CHECK

Draw Conclusions **Is this book a primary or a secondary source?**

Introduction Review and Assess

Vocabulary

Number a paper from 1 to 8. Beside each number, write the word from the list that matches the description.

environment   climate   census
citizen   economy   culture
supply and demand   artifact

1. A region's weather pattern over a number of years

2. Shared language, beliefs, and customs

3. The living and nonliving things that surround us

4. A population count

5. Someone born in a country or who becomes a member by law

6. Forces that determine the selling price of goods

7. The way a country uses its natural resources, money, and knowledge to produce good and services

8. Human-made product such as pottery, clothing, and tools

Comprehension and Critical Thinking

Write a sentence to answer each question.

9. **Geography** How is a plateau different from a basin?

10. **Critical Thinking** Is drinking water a renewable or a nonrenewable resource?

11. **Government** Why did the founders of the United States decide to take a census?

12. **Critical Thinking** Why does the United States Constitution protect the freedom of religion?

13. **Economy** What services do people pay for with taxes?

14. **Critical Thinking** Why does the price of gasoline usually rise at a certain time of year, such as summer, when people do a great deal of traveling?

15. **History** How do families create oral histories?

16. **Critical Thinking** How do artifacts help historians understand a culture?

Illinois Standards Achievement Test Preparation

In 1787 representatives from 12 of the 13 states created the United States Constitution. The delegates decided that the Constitution should begin with a single sentence called a Preamble. The Preamble states,

"We the People of the United States, in Order to form a more perfect Union, establish Justice, insure domestic Tranquility [peace at home], provide for the common Defense, promote the general Welfare, and secure the blessing of Liberty to ourselves and our Posterity [future generations] do ordain [create] and establish this constitution for the United States of America."

1

The suffix *pre-* in the word preamble means—

Ⓐ after.
Ⓑ before.
Ⓒ early.
Ⓓ late.

2

What is another way to say "promote the general welfare?"

Ⓐ Allow only some people to vote
Ⓑ Pay lawmakers to serve in Congress
Ⓒ Hire people to work for the government
Ⓓ Help all Americans

3

A person would read the Preamble of the Constitution to—

Ⓐ learn their rights as a U.S. citizen.
Ⓑ find out about the lives of the forefathers.
Ⓒ understand the purpose of the Constitution.
Ⓓ gather information about the powers of the President.

4

How many states were there in 1787?

Ⓐ Twelve
Ⓑ zero
Ⓒ Two
Ⓓ Thirteen

The Big Idea # Activities

> What can places, people, and ideas tells us about the United States?

Write About the Big Idea

Use the completed Overview Foldable to write an expository essay that answers the Big Idea question: *What can places, people, and ideas tell us about the United States?* Write three separate paragraphs on places, people, and ideas. In the first sentence of each paragraph, write the main idea. Write at least two more sentences with details to support your main idea.

 FOLDABLES™ Study Organizer

United States

| Places | People | Ideas |

Make a Scrapbook

Make a scrapbook about your town or city. Find or draw pictures that show:

- the region you live in
- the ecosystem where you live
- some natural resources in your area
- government buildings in your town
- an important part of your town's economy
- an important historical place or event in your town

When you have put together the scrapbook, choose a title for the book. Then find or draw one picture that says the most about your town or city.

Washington, D.C.

REGION: Middle Atlantic States
ECOSYSTEM: Urban and Suburban
NATURAL
RESOURCES: Fish, Woodlands

GOVERNMENT
BUILDING: White House
MAIN EMPLOYER: Federal government

BIG EVENT: Presidential
                           Inauguration

The Ancestral Pueblo built their homes into the sides of cliffs at Mesa Verde.

Essential Question
How do people adapt to where they live?

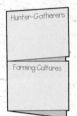

FOLDABLES™
Study Organizer

Compare and Contrast
Make and label a Two-tab Foldable book before you read this unit. Label the tabs **Hunter-Gatherers** and **Farming Cultures**. Use the Foldable to organize information as you read.

Hunter-Gatherers

Farming Cultures

LOG ON
For more about Unit 1 go to www.macmillanmh.com

NATIVE PEOPLES OF NORTH AMERICA

PEOPLE, PLACES, AND EVENTS

Maya Artifact

Navajo Woman

Central America

250 | Maya cities arise in Mexico and Guatemala

Southwest

1200 | Navajo settle in the Southwest

200   400   600   800

In about A.D. 250, **Maya** cities arose in the rain forests of Mexico and **Central America**.

Today you can visit ruins of ancient Maya cities such as Tikal and Chichén Itzá.

The **Navajo** people settled in the **Southwest** in about A.D. 1200.

Today the Navajo follow many of their traditional customs.

LOG ON

For more about People, Places, and Events, visit
www.macmillanmh.com

Mississippian Artifact

Iroquois Chief

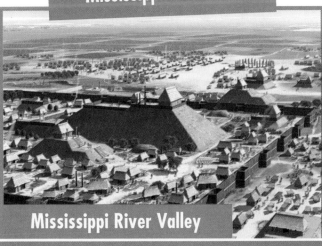

Mississippi River Valley

1300 | Cahokia is abandoned

Northeast

1451 | Iroquois Confederacy adopts early constitution

1000   1200   1400   1600

Cahokia, a large city built by **Mississippian Mound Builders**, was deserted by about 1300.

Today you can see Cahokia's largest mounds at a park near Collinsville, Illinois.

In 1451 the five nations of the **Iroquois Confederacy** adopted the "**Great Law of Peace**," an early constitution.

Today many members of the Confederacy live in New York.

Settling the Americas

Lesson 1

VOCABULARY

archaeologist p. 21

glacier p. 21

civilization p. 22

irrigation p. 24

adobe p. 24

READING SKILL

Compare and Contrast
Copy the chart below. As you read, fill it in with facts about the Ancestral Pueblo and the people of Cahokia.

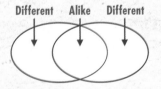

Different   Alike   Different

Illinois Learning Standards

15.D.2b, 16.B.2a (W), 16.C.2a (W), 16.C.2b (W), 17.C.2b, 17.C.2c, 17.D.2a, 18.C.2

Hunter-gatherers attack an Ice Age mastodon.

Visual Preview

How did early people adapt to life in North America?

A Hunter-gatherers followed animals into North America by land and water.

B The Olmec and Maya developed farming in Mexico and Central America.

C The Hohokam, Ancestral Pueblo, and Mound Builders settled in North America.

D The people of Cahokia built a large agricultural society in North America.

A THE FIRST HUNTER-GATHERERS

Suppose you had to travel a long distance thousands of years ago, and you could only paddle along a coastline or walk across land. What plants and animals might you eat along the way? There were no grocery stores, so you would have to find your own food.

The first Native Americans followed animals that supplied their food and clothing. When animals moved, people moved after them. In some regions a hunting trip could take days, so people ate a lot of plants. They gathered wild berries, mushrooms, and grasses. That's why we call them hunter-gatherers.

Archaeologists are people who study the tools, bones, and remains of ancient people. Some archaeologists think that hunter-gatherers first reached North America from Asia between 15,000 and 30,000 years ago. No one can say for sure when the first people arrived in the Americas.

Coastal and Land Routes

During the Ice Age, water froze into thick sheets of slow-moving ice called **glaciers**. Glaciers held so much water that ocean levels dropped and land appeared in some places. Over time, a land bridge appeared that joined Asia and the Americas. We call this the Beringia Land Bridge.

Many archaeologists believe the first people to arrive in North America crossed the land bridge from Asia and followed a water route along the Pacific Ocean. Archaeologists have found remains that show people may have reached the tip of South America. Other hunter-gatherers arrived in North America from Asia about 12,000 years ago. Archaeologists believe these early humans settled across the Americas.

QUICK CHECK

Compare and Contrast How were the lives of hunter-gatherers different from the lives of people today?

▼ Archaeologists study remains at a settlement of early people in South America.

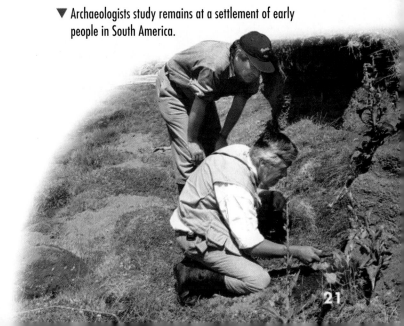

About 10,000 B.C. the last Ice Age ended, and Earth's climate grew warmer. Ice Age mammals, such as mammoths and mastodons, could not survive in warmer weather. Humans had to start growing food when they could not hunt or gather enough to survive.

No one knows how farming first started. We do know that in the Americas it started in Mexico. By about 7000 B.C., people in Mexico and Central America were raising three crops: maize (also called corn), beans, and squash.

As in the Fertile Crescent of Asia, farmers in the Americas produced surpluses—more food than they needed. Some people now were free to specialize. They became traders, builders, or potters, for example. Over time, large specialized societies developed and became **civilizations** —populations that shared systems of trade, art, religion, and science.

The Olmec

In about 1200 B.C., the Olmec civilization developed in the steamy rain forests of southern Mexico. Olmec culture spread along trade routes across Mexico and Central America. One of the wealthiest centers of the Olmec was La Venta, which produced rubber, tar, and salt. La Venta had a large

▼ This Maya pyramid, the Temple of Five Stories, is located in Mexico.

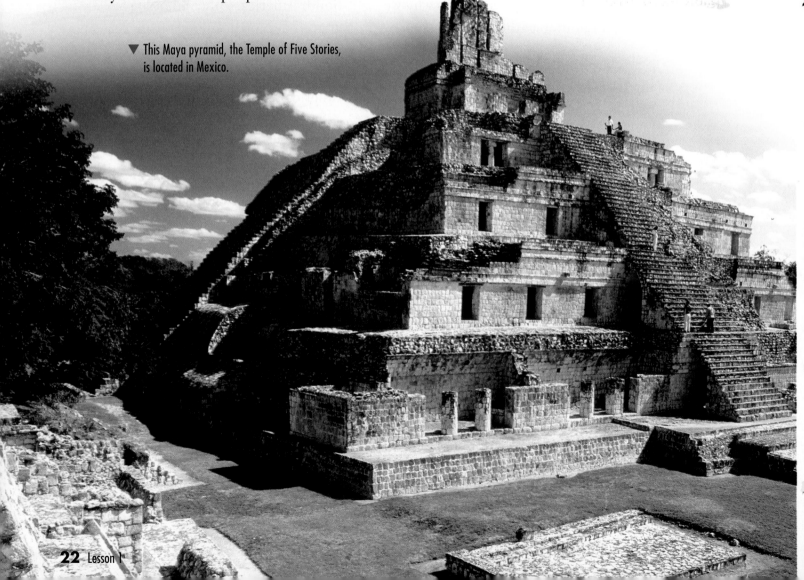

fishing industry. Its people were the first to make food from a wild bean known as *cacao*—chocolate. Today the Olmec culture is famous for enormous stone head carvings found in Mexico. The Olmec also developed a calendar and were likely the first American people to understand the concept of zero.

The Maya

In about 2600 B.C., the Maya arose in the same region as the Olmec. Both groups settled in southeastern Mexico and Central America. From about A.D. 250 to 900, the Maya became a powerful civilization. Like the Olmec, the Maya had scientists who created calendars and studied the stars. The Maya also developed a system of mathematics and a form of writing called hieroglyphs.

The Maya were talented artists and builders. Workers built stone pyramids and temples to honor their hundreds of gods. These buildings can still be seen today. The Maya also built stone palaces, roads, and ball courts. Maya cities such as Chichén Itzá, Tikal, and Copán had populations of several thousand people.

Over time, the population outgrew the food supply. People moved out of the cities in search of food. The Maya civilization lost power by A.D. 900, but the people did not disappear. Today more than 6 million Maya live in Mexico, Belize, and Guatemala.

QUICK CHECK

Compare and Contrast **How were the Olmec and Maya alike?**

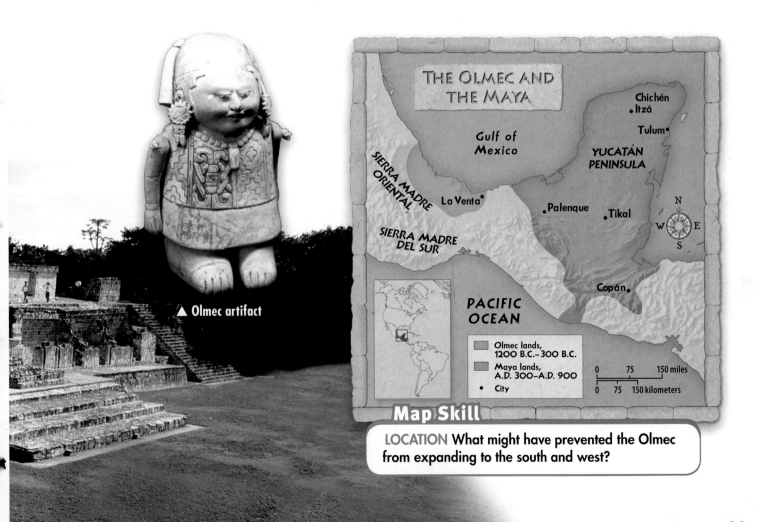

▲ Olmec artifact

THE OLMEC AND THE MAYA

Chichén Itzá

Tulum

Gulf of Mexico

YUCATÁN PENINSULA

SIERRA MADRE ORIENTAL

La Venta

Palenque

Tikal

N
W   E
S

SIERRA MADRE DEL SUR

Copán

PACIFIC OCEAN

Olmec lands, 1200 B.C.–300 B.C.
Maya lands, A.D. 300–A.D. 900
• City

0   75   150 miles
0   75   150 kilometers

Map Skill

LOCATION **What might have prevented the Olmec from expanding to the south and west?**

23

If you could go back thousands of years and fly over southwest North America, you would see narrow waterways flowing through the desert and cities built into cliffs. If you could fly over the Mississippi River valley, you would see large round hills built by humans.

The Hohokam

In about A.D. 300, a group known as the Hohokam settled in the desert of present-day Arizona. The Hohokam grew maize, beans, squash, and cotton in this hot, dry region. How did they do it? They used **irrigation** to guide water from rivers to their fields. Irrigation supplies dry land with water through pipes and ditches. Using sharpened sticks and stone hoes, Hohokam workers dug canals, or human-made waterways, to carry water many miles.

The Hohokam also trapped rabbits, birds, and snakes. They ate wild desert plants, such as cactus and prickly pear.

With little stone or wood for building, the Hohokam built homes from **adobe**—bricks made of mud and straw. These homes were built partly underground in pits. Building underground helped to keep the homes cool during the day and warm at night.

Ancestral Pueblo

In about A.D. 700, a people called the Ancestral Pueblo settled in the Southwest. They lived in dwellings that looked like apartment buildings built into the sides of cliffs. These dwellings had special rooms called kivas for meetings or religious purposes.

▼ The Taos Pueblo is located in New Mexico.

Adena Artifact

The **Adena** of the Ohio River valley were the first mound builders. The earliest mounds were tombs. The dead were placed in log rooms in the mounds. Tools and other items for use in the next world were placed beside the body.

The natural world was the center of Ancestral Pueblo beliefs. Historian John Upton Terrell said,

> **❝**The [Ancestral Pueblo] see themselves as woven into . . . the winds, the stars, and the moon. . . .**❞**

Like the Hohokam, the Ancestral Pueblo planted maize, beans, and squash. They used dry farming, a method that caught rain and melted snow in stone-lined pits. They then used this water on their crops.

Mound Builders

Other North American civilizations developed in river valleys of the Midwest. Over a period of about 1,000 years, civilizations arose in the Ohio and Mississippi River valleys. The people are called mound builders because of the cone-shaped hills and animal-shaped earthworks they built.

In about 200 B.C., the Hopewell were the first civilization to settle in the Mississippi River valley. Many Hopewell mounds can be seen today across the Midwest. Some were burial mounds, and others were used for religious ceremonies.

Another civilization, called the Mississippian culture, developed in about A.D. 700. Like the other mound-building cultures, they buried their dead in mounds. They also used their mounds as places to watch the movements of the sun and stars.

QUICK CHECK

Compare and Contrast How were the shelters of the Hohokam and Ancestral Pueblo different?

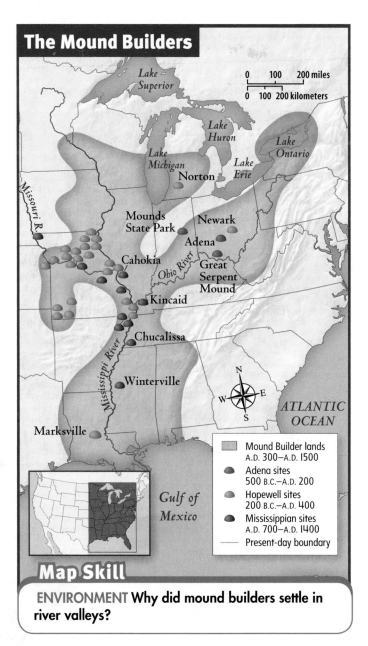

The Mound Builders

0   100   200 miles
0   100   200 kilometers

Lake Superior
Lake Huron
Lake Michigan
Lake Erie
Lake Ontario
Missouri R.
Norton
Mounds State Park
Newark
Adena
Cahokia
Ohio River
Great Serpent Mound
Kincaid
Chucalissa
Mississippi River
Winterville
Marksville
ATLANTIC OCEAN
Gulf of Mexico

☐ Mound Builder lands
A.D. 300–A.D. 1500
● Adena sites
500 B.C.–A.D. 200
● Hopewell sites
200 B.C.–A.D. 400
● Mississippian sites
A.D. 700–A.D. 1400
— Present-day boundary

Map Skill

ENVIRONMENT Why did mound builders settle in river valleys?

The greatest Mississippian city was Cahokia, built near present-day St. Louis, Missouri. By A.D. 1100 Cahokia's population was about 20,000, making it one of the largest cities in the world at the time. Villages stretched around the city in all directions. High log fences, called palisades, protected the villages.

Like other agricultural societies, the people of Cahokia needed to know about the patterns of the seasons. Archaeologists have found the remains of a great circle of tree trunks outside Cahokia. They believe farmers planted these to act as a giant sundial.

Scientists do not agree about what happened to the people of Cahokia. Some say climate change, wars, or disease may have driven people out of the city. By 1300, Cahokia was empty.

QUICK CHECK

Compare and Contrast How did the Adena, Hopewell, and Mississippian peoples use earth mounds?

▼ Cahokia was one of the largest cities in the world in A.D. 1100.

Check Understanding

1. **VOCABULARY** Write a sentence about people who study ancient groups. Use three of the vocabulary terms below.

   archaeologist civilization adobe

   glacier irrigation

2. **READING SKILL Compare and Contrast** Use your chart from page 20 to write a paragraph comparing the Ancestral Pueblo with the people of Cahokia.

3. **Write About It** Write a paragraph that tells how the Hohokam adapted to their environment.

EXPLORE The Big Idea

Chart and Graph Skills

Read Parallel Time Lines

VOCABULARY

time line

B.C.

A.D.

B.C.E.

C.E.

century

circa

parallel time line

A **time line** lists events in history. Some time lines use the abbreviation **B.C.** It stands for "before Christ." The letters **A.D.** are for years after the birth of Christ. Some time lines use **B.C.E.**, which stands for "before the Common Era," and **C.E.**, which means "common era." Time lines can be divided into time periods. A **century**, or 100 years, is one time period. The word **circa** means "around" or "about." It is used when an exact date is not known.

The time line below is a **parallel time line**. Parallel time lines show two sets of dates and events on the same time line.

Learn It

Read the parallel time line below.

● The time line begins in the year 1500 B.C. and ends at A.D. 1000.

● The Olmec events took place in 1300 B.C., 900 B.C., and 300 B.C. The Maya events happened in 800 B.C., 300 B.C., A.D. 250, A.D. 500, and A.D. 900.

Try It

Use the time line to answer the questions.

● Which culture developed first, the Olmec or the Maya? Explain your answer.

● Which events on the time line happened around the same time?

Apply It

● Make a time line of your life. Then add events that have taken place in the United States during your lifetime.

Parallel Time Line: Early Peoples of North America

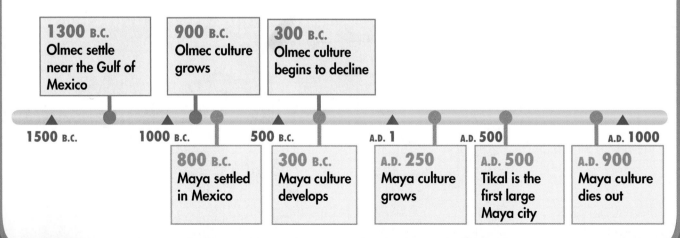

1300 B.C. Olmec settle near the Gulf of Mexico

900 B.C. Olmec culture grows

300 B.C. Olmec culture begins to decline

1500 B.C. 1000 B.C. 500 B.C. A.D. 1 A.D. 500 A.D. 1000

800 B.C. Maya settled in Mexico

300 B.C. Maya culture develops

A.D. 250 Maya culture grows

A.D. 500 Tikal is the first large Maya city

A.D. 900 Maya culture dies out

NATIVE AMERICANS OF THE WEST

VOCABULARY

totem pole p. 30

potlatch p. 31

READING SKILL

Compare and Contrast
Copy the chart below. As you read, use it to compare and contrast the Inuit and Tlingit.

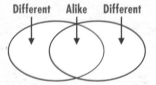

Different   Alike   Different

Illinois Learning Standards

17.B.2a, 17.B.2b, 17.B.2c, 17.C.2a, 17.C.2b, 17.C.2c, 17.D.2a, 18.C.2

Whales were important to Native American economies in the West.

Visual Preview

How did the environments of the West affect the lives of Native Americans?

A The Inuit hunted whales to use for food, tools, weapons, and cooking oil.

B The Tlingit used nearby forests to make canoes, totem poles, and masks.

A VARIED LANDS AND PEOPLE

For Native Americans in the West, environment helped form culture. The West is a region of great diversity—from the extreme cold of the Arctic to the hot, dry deserts of southern California. Cultures developed according to the climate and natural resources of the surroundings.

The Inuit in Alaska had to find ways to live in the bitterly cold Arctic. They kept warm by building pit houses made of stone and covered with earth. When they went on hunting trips, men built igloos, temporary shelters of snow blocks. In warm weather, hunters made tents from wooden poles and animal skins. The Inuit hunted walruses, seals, fish, and whales. They used the skins for clothing and turned bones into tools and weapons.

The California Desert

Life in the desert of southern California was different from life in the Arctic. Groups such as the Cahuilla and Paiute used desert plants, including roots and cactus berries, for food. They also grew crops using irrigation. The Cahuilla, for example, dug wells in the desert sand and packed sand around the wells, creating small lakes. They used the lakes to water fields of maize, squash, beans, and melons.

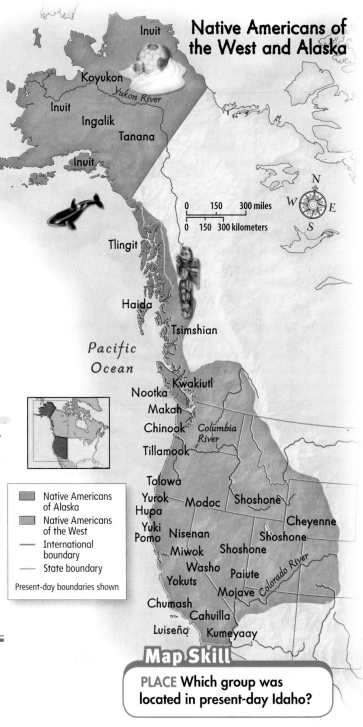

Native Americans of the West and Alaska

Inuit
Koyukon
Yukon River
Inuit
Ingalik
Tanana
Inuit
Tlingit
Haida
Tsimshian
Pacific Ocean
Kwakiutl
Nootka
Makah
Chinook — Columbia River
Tillamook
Tolowa
Yurok — Modoc — Shoshone
Hupa
Yuki — Cheyenne
Pomo — Nisenan — Shoshone
Miwok — Shoshone
Washo
Yokuts — Paiute — Colorado River
Mojave
Chumash
Cahuilla
Luiseño — Kumeyaay

Native Americans of Alaska
Native Americans of the West
—— International boundary
—— State boundary
Present-day boundaries shown

N W E S
0   150   300 miles
0   150   300 kilometers

QUICK CHECK

Compare and Contrast How are the Inuit different from Native Americans of the California desert?

Map Skill

PLACE **Which group was located in present-day Idaho?**

29

Like Native Americans in other regions, those in the Pacific Northwest used only enough plants and animals to survive. The region was rich in natural resources, so its groups often did not need to farm. The rocky, narrow coastline and offshore islands of this region provided wild plants and fish, especially salmon.

Native Americans used stone axes to cut fir and cedar trees. They hollowed out logs to make canoes as long as 60 feet—perfect for hunting seals and whales in the Pacific Ocean. Logs were also carved into boxes, dishes, spoons, and masks.

Celebrations

Pacific Northwest groups also used wood to make **totem poles**. Totem poles are carved logs that are painted with symbols, called totems, of animals or people. Totem poles often told stories of important family members or celebrated special events.

Potlatch dancer

Citizenship

Be a Leader

Have you ever thought of being a leader? In 1945 Tlingit civil rights leader Elizabeth Peratrovich was responsible for a civil rights law that gave Native Americans equal rights. Leaders are able to identify problems and find solutions. Consider being a leader in your community or school.

Write About It Identify a problem in your community or school. Then write an essay about how you would work with others to find a solution.

The Tlingit continue to use the abundant resources of the sea and forests. Tlingit women are known around the world for their fine baskets made from cedar trees. Tlingit men continue the traditional wood carving and painting of totem poles, canoes, and face masks.

Tlingit carver

When totem poles were raised, a family sometimes held a **potlatch**. Potlatches are special feasts at which guests, not hosts, receive gifts. The host might give hundreds of gifts at the feast, which could last for several days. In return, the host received the respect of the community. As in the past, potlatches today bring people together for important family events such as the birth, death, or marriage of a family member.

The Wealth of the Tlingit

The Tlingit settled in the Pacific Northwest. Like other people in the region, they got most of their food and goods from the sea. The Tlingit traveled by canoe to trade their surplus, or extra, goods with other groups along the coast. This extensive system of trade made the Tlingit wealthy. In the 1700s the Tlingit lived in an area that stretched about 400 miles along the coast between Mount St. Elias in southeastern Alaska and what is now the Portland Canal in British Columbia. The Pacific Ocean's warm North Pacific Current kept the

weather mild and wet. These conditions made it easy to get food and wood, so the Tlingit often had free time to develop trades and crafts.

The Tlingit used this time to become skilled craftworkers. They used tree bark and other materials to weave colorful blankets and made sturdy baskets. The Tlingit also built wooden plank houses large enough to hold several related families. Totem poles stood in front of some houses. The Tlingit still live in Alaska today.

QUICK CHECK

Compare and Contrast How was the way the Tlingit adapted to their environment different from other Native American groups?

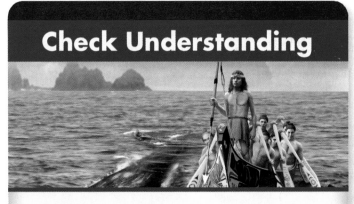

Check Understanding

1. **VOCABULARY** Write a sentence for each vocabulary term below.

   totem pole   potlatch

2. **READING SKILL Compare and Contrast** Use your chart from page 28 to write about the Inuit and Tlingit.

Different   Alike   Different

3. **Write About It** Write about how geography affected the lives of Native Americans in the West.

VOCABULARY

migrate p. 34

hogan p. 35

READING SKILL

Compare and Contrast
Copy the chart below. As you read, use it to compare and contrast the Pueblo and Navajo.

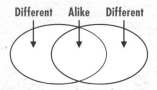

Different   Alike   Different

Illinois Learning Standards

17.B.2a, 17.B.2b, 17.B.2c,
17.C.2a, 17.C.2b, 17.C.2c,
17.D.2a, 18.C.2

PEOPLE OF THE SOUTHWEST

A Pueblo deer dance celebration

Visual Preview

How did the desert environment affect people's lives?

A Pueblos are made of adobe, which protects the homes from extreme heat and cold.

B The Navajo learned how to use sheep for food and wool.

A THE PUEBLO

The Ancestral Pueblo you read about in lesson one are believed to be related to later Pueblo groups. Like their ancestors, the Pueblo had to adapt to where they lived to survive.

Can you imagine farming in a place that receives only a few inches of rain each year? The Pueblo—like their ancestors—figured out how to farm in the desert. They used a method called dry farming.

The Amazing Pueblo Farmers

Dry farming uses tiny dams and canals to direct water to beans, squash, and cotton crops. The Pueblo also learned how to grow a special maize plant with long roots that could reach water deep underground. The Hopi and Zuni are two Pueblo groups shown on the map below.

PLACES

The **Taos Pueblo** is over 1,000 years old. The multistoried buildings are made of adobe. Today you can visit the Taos Pueblo where shops sell pottery, silver jewelry, and leather goods.

Taos Pueblo

Pueblo Homes

The Pueblo built homes called pueblos out of adobe. The Spanish used the word pueblo to describe both the people and their homes. Adobe protects homes from extreme heat or cold. Pueblos looked like apartment buildings, except that the first floor of most pueblos had no doors or windows. To get in and out of a pueblo, people climbed a ladder to a door in the roof. By lifting the ladder up and placing it on the roof, they were protected from unwanted guests.

Native Americans of the Southwest, 1700s

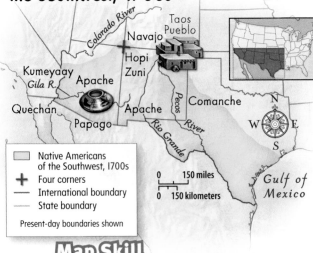

Colorado River
Taos Pueblo
Navajo
Hopi
Zuni
Kumeyaay
Gila R.
Apache
Quechan
Papago
Apache
Pecos River
Comanche
Rio Grande
N W E S
Gulf of Mexico

Native Americans of the Southwest, 1700s
+ Four corners
International boundary
State boundary
Present-day boundaries shown

0   150 miles
0   150 kilometers

Map Skill

LOCATION **Which rivers are on or near Apache lands?**

QUICK CHECK

Compare and Contrast **How were the Pueblo similar to the Ancestral Pueblo?**

B THE NAVAJO

Thousands of years ago, the Navajo, or Diné, were hunter-gatherers in parts of present-day Alaska and Canada. The Navajo began to **migrate**, or move, to northern New Mexico by the late 1200s.

Today the Navajo are the largest non-Pueblo people in the Southwest. Many live in the Four Corners area, where the states of Utah, Colorado, Arizona, and New Mexico meet.

Learning from the Pueblo

In order to survive, the Navajo knew they had to adapt ideas and practices from their Pueblo neighbors. Like the Pueblo, the Navajo used dry farming to grow crops in the dry land. They also wove cotton to make cloth. Both the Navajo and the Pueblo are known for their fine silver and turquoise jewelry. Turquoise is a blue stone that is found only in the Southwest and in western South America.

◀ A Navajo grandmother teaches her granddaughter how to weave a blanket.

Navajo hogan ➡

Navajo Living

The Navajo lived in **hogans**, which are dome-shaped homes for one family. The hogans are made with log or stick frames that are covered with mud or sod. They have a smoke hole in the roof to release the smoke from a fire. Traditional hogans have six or eight sides and face east to catch the first rays of dawn.

The Navajo captured sheep from the Spaniards in the 1600s. These animals became an important part of Navajo culture. Many Navajo people became shepherds. The meat provided food, and weavers made wool into clothes and blankets.

The Navajo believed in a balance to the Earth that they called *hozho*, or "walking in beauty." To maintain hozho, the Navajo sing songs or chants. One song says, "All is beautiful before me, All is beautiful behind me, All is beautiful above me, All is beautiful around me."

QUICK CHECK

Compare and Contrast **In what ways are pueblos different from hogans?**

▲ Turquoise squash blossom necklace

Check Understanding

1. **VOCABULARY** Write about the Navajo using these vocabulary words.

   migrate   **hogan**

2. **READING SKILL Compare and Contrast** Use your chart from page 32 to write about the Pueblo and Navajo.

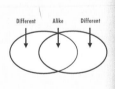

3. **Write About It** Write about how the Pueblo or Navajo learned to live in the Southwest.

35

Lesson 4

VOCABULARY

teepee p. 37

lodge p. 37

travois p. 38

coup stick p. 39

READING SKILL

Compare and Contrast
Copy the chart below. As you read, use it to compare and contrast life on the Plains before and after the arrival of horses.

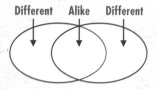

Illinois Learning Standards

17.B.2a, 17.B.2b, 17.B.2c, 17.C.2a, 17.C.2b, 17.C.2c, 17.D.2a, 18.C.2

NATIVE AMERICANS OF THE PLAINS

This painting shows the excitement of a buffalo hunt.

Visual Preview

How did the natural resources of the Plains impact Native Americans?

A Hunting bison provided food, clothing, and shelter.

B During the winter, the Lakota made clothing, tools, and calendars.

THE OPEN PLAINS

Imagine looking into the distance, seeing only land and blue sky. The Great Plains is a vast, nearly flat region where you can see for miles. The land has powerful winds, blistering summer heat, and cold winters.

Native Americans began to settle on the Great Plains in about 1300. They hunted for food on foot. They used bows and arrows and stampeded animals into traps. Some groups farmed near rivers.

Horses Arrive

By the 1700s, wild horses had spread from the Southwest to the Great Plains. Once tamed, they changed the lives of people there. Men hunted on horseback, and many groups traded with faraway groups. As a result, groups such as the Lakota, Crow, Pawnee, and Cheyenne prospered on the Plains.

Where the Bison Roam

Between 40 million and 100 million bison roamed the Great Plains in the 1700s. They provided food and clothing. Some groups used bison skin to make **teepees**. Teepees are cone-shaped homes made with long poles covered with animal hides.

Some Plains groups stayed in one place and lived in large earthen **lodges**. Lodges are homes made of logs covered with grasses, sticks, and soil. A fire in a central fireplace provided heat and light.

QUICK CHECK

Compare and Contrast In what ways are teepees different from lodges?

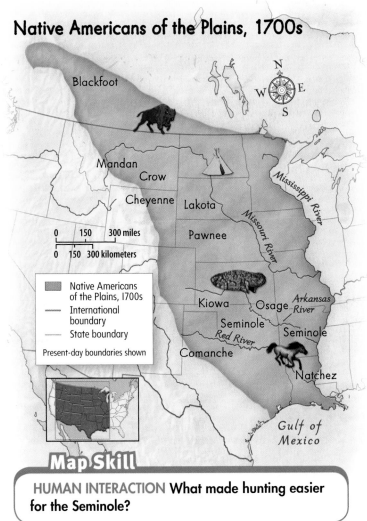

Native Americans of the Plains, 1700s

Blackfoot

Mandan

Crow

Cheyenne

Lakota

Pawnee

Missouri River

Mississippi River

0 150 300 miles
0 150 300 kilometers

■ Native Americans of the Plains, 1700s
— International boundary
— State boundary
Present-day boundaries shown

Kiowa Osage Arkansas River

Seminole Red River Seminole

Comanche

Natchez

Gulf of Mexico

Map Skill

HUMAN INTERACTION What made hunting easier for the Seminole?

Fire was not only used to cook bison meat, it was also used in the hunt. Some hunters often set grass fires to frighten a herd into a stampede. Often hundreds of animals would rush over a cliff, falling to their deaths. The hunters would then gather the meat and skins that they needed. Plains people used a **travois** to carry the meat and skins back to camp.

A travois is a sled-like device that is dragged by people or animals. At first, dogs were trained to pull the travois. Later, horses did the job.

Keeping Records

Would you go outside if it was 20 degrees below zero? The Lakota did not. Instead they used the long, cold winter months to stay close to a fire. There they made clothes, weapons, or tools. They also made illustrated calendars called winter counts.

When the Lakota settled in a camp for the winter, they met to decide the most important events of that year. These events were painted as picture symbols in a circle on bison hide. The history of the Lakota is read counter-clockwise, moving left, from the center of the circle. Study the winter count on this page.

Primary Sources

This winter count was created by a Lakota named Lone Dog. It is a copy of the original, which was destroyed in a fire. The symbols are read in a counter-clockwise spiral. The key tells the meaning of some of the symbols. How does the winter count help you understand Lone Dog's life?

An 1800–1871 Winter Count by Lone Dog

 1800–1801
Europeans bring striped blankets

 1845–1846
30 Lakota killed by Crow Indians

 1845–1846
There is plenty of meat

Write About It Write a journal entry giving more details about an event shown on the winter count.

The **Spanish brought horses** with them to North America in the 1500s. Some horses got away and lived in the wild. In the 1600s, the Pueblo were using horses in the Southwest. By the 1700s horses had moved into the Great Plains, forever changing the lives of the people who lived there.

Horses arrive

In most Plains cultures, a child's first success was given public recognition. For example, Blackfoot boys who won shooting matches were allowed to wear feathers in their hair like older men. Children were also praised for showing qualities that were admired, such as being generous and speaking well.

QUICK CHECK

Compare and Contrast Why were the skills taught to boys different from those taught to girls?

Learning Life Skills

Parents taught their children useful skills early in life. On the Great Plains, parents taught their children good listening skills by telling them stories and singing songs about their culture. Boys were taught to hunt and shoot. They learned, for example, to track small game such as rabbits and birds. They used small bows and arrows to shoot these moving targets. Later they took part in shooting matches and practice battles. Boys also learned the value of courage. One way they showed courage was to touch an enemy without killing him. To do this, they used a special pole called a **coup stick**. Coup is the French word for "strike" or "hit."

Girls learned different skills. They learned to sew by making doll clothes, using the sinews from bison as thread. Sinews are tendons that connect muscle to bone. Girls were also given toy teepees to set up while their mothers set up the family teepees. Older girls learned how to use scraping tools to clean animal skins. The skills taught to children on the Great Plains would prepare them for different tasks as adults.

Check Understanding

1. **VOCABULARY** Write a story about a day in a village of Native Americans on the Great Plains using the vocabulary terms below.

   teepee   travois
   lodge   coup stick

2. **READING SKILL** Compare and Contrast Use your chart from page 36 to write about Plains groups.

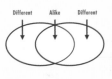

Different   Alike   Different

EXPLORE The Big Idea

3. **Write About It** How did Native Americans on the Great Plains adapt to the environment?

VOCABULARY

slash-and-burn p. 41

longhouse p. 43

wampum p. 43

Creek Confederacy p. 44

clan p. 44

Iroquois Confederacy p. 45

READING SKILL

Compare and Contrast
Copy the chart below. As you read, use it to compare and contrast the Iroquois and the Creek.

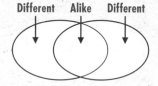

Different   Alike   Different

Illinois Learning Standards
17.B.2a, 17.B.2b, 17.B.2c, 17.C.2a, 17.C.2b, 17.C.2c, 17.D.2a, 18.C.2

People of the Eastern Woodlands

An Iroquois man dances outside a reconstructed longhouse.

Visual Preview

How did the environment shape Eastern Woodlands cultures?

A People hunted forest animals and grew maize, squash, and beans.

B The Iroquois used materials from the forests to build their homes.

C Groups worked together to protect and govern themselves.

A   A LAND RICH IN FORESTS

Did you know that North America was once called Turtle Island?
The Iroquois named it that because they believed Sky Woman fell out
of the sky and the Great Turtle caught her, causing an island to form.

The Iroquois include five groups, the Cayuga, the Mohawk, the Oneida, the Onondaga, and the Seneca. These groups share many cultural traits, such as language. When the Iroquois settled in present-day New York, the area was covered with thick forests. They said the forests were so thick that a squirrel could jump from tree to tree for a thousand miles without touching the ground. Forest animals, such as deer, provided woodland groups with food and clothing.

Farming the Land

Because the forests were so thick, many groups in the Eastern Woodlands practiced a type of farming called **slash-and-burn**. They cut down, or slashed, trees. They then burned the undergrowth to clear room for crops. Ash from the burned vegetation helped to make the soil fertile. After a crop had been harvested, they left the plot empty for several years. The next year another plot was cleared and planted. This method helped keep the soil from wearing out.

Each spring most groups planted the "Three Sisters" of maize, squash, and beans. In autumn crops were harvested, dried, and stored for the winter.

QUICK CHECK

Compare and Contrast **Compare slash-and-burn farming with dry farming.**

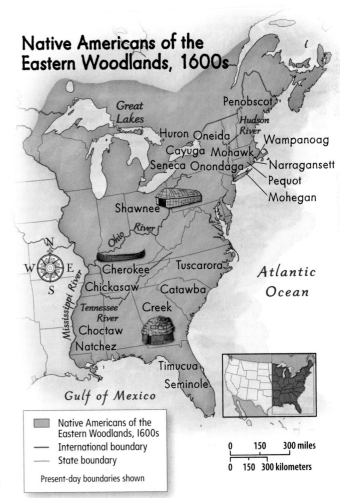

Native Americans of the Eastern Woodlands, 1600s

Great Lakes · Penobscot · Huron · Oneida · Hudson River · Wampanoag · Cayuga · Mohawk · Seneca · Onondaga · Narragansett · Pequot · Mohegan · Shawnee · Ohio River · N W E S · Mississippi River · Cherokee · Tuscarora · Atlantic Ocean · Chickasaw · Catawba · Tennessee River · Creek · Choctaw · Natchez · Timucua · Seminole · Gulf of Mexico

Native Americans of the Eastern Woodlands, 1600s
— International boundary
— State boundary
Present-day boundaries shown

0   150   300 miles
0   150 300 kilometers

Map Skill

LOCATION Which river created a natural boundary for Native Americans of the Eastern Woodlands?

41

THE CREEK AND IROQUOIS

Archaeologists believe the Creek of the southern woodlands are descendants of the Mississippian mound-building people. When a Creek town reached a population of about 400 to 600 people, about half the population would move to a new site.

CREEK

Creek Villages

▶ The Creek (known as the Muskogee today) arranged their towns around a large council house or "Chokofa." Family homes were wattle-and-daub huts, which are made from poles and covered with grass, mud, or thatch.

Creek Art

▶ The Creek decorated their pots with wooden stamps. They pressed the carved stamps into pottery while it was still wet.

Celebrations

▶ Both the Creek and Iroquois celebrated the Green Corn Festival, honoring the summer's first maize crop.

The Iroquois of the northern woodlands usually built their villages on the tops of steep-sided hills. The steep slopes formed natural defenses for the village. A high log fence was commonly built along the edge of a village for added protection.

QUICK CHECK

Compare and Contrast **How are Creek and Iroquois villages different?**

IROQUOIS

Iroquois Villages

▶ The Iroquois call themselves Hodenosaunee. In Iroquoian this means "people of the **longhouse**." Longhouses were large enough for several families and were made of bent poles covered with sheets of bark. The longest longhouse is thought to have been 334 feet. That's longer than a football field!

Iroquois Art

▶ The Iroquois made fine beadwork, called **wampum**. Wampum is polished beads made from shells that are woven together. It was used in ceremonies or as gifts.

Sports

▶ Both the Iroquois and the Creek played lacrosse. lacrosse sometimes settled disagreements among groups.

GOVERNMENT IN THE WOODLANDS

Archaeologists group Native Americans in many ways. One way is by language. Find the language family of the Creek in the chart on this page. Native Americans can also be grouped by how they governed themselves. Some groups formed confederacies. A confederacy is a union of people who join together for a common purpose.

Creek Government

To protect themselves from enemies, the Creek formed the **Creek Confederacy**. Most of the groups in the confederacy spoke Muskogean languages. The groups also shared customs, such as the Green Corn Festival.

The Creek Confederacy divided its towns into war towns (red) and peace towns (white). Red towns declared war, planned battles, and held meetings with enemy groups. White towns passed laws and held prisoners. During periods of war, however, even people in peace towns joined in the fighting. When a new town formed, it maintained close ties to other towns. This kept the Creek Confederacy united.

Iroquois Society

Iroquois women were leaders of their society and did most of the farming. They decided how land would be used and who would use it. Women were the heads of their **clans**. A clan is a group of families that share the same ancestor. The head of each clan was called a clan mother. No important decision could be made without the approval of the clan mother. Although the leaders of each village were men, it was the clan mothers who chose them—and could also remove them.

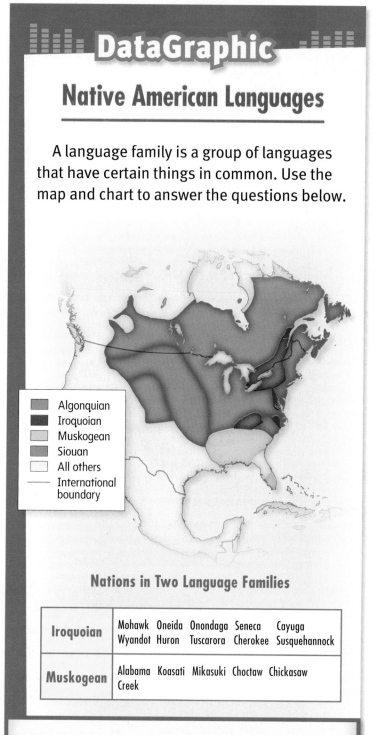

DataGraphic

Native American Languages

A language family is a group of languages that have certain things in common. Use the map and chart to answer the questions below.

Legend:
- Algonquian
- Iroquoian
- Muskogean
- Siouan
- All others
- International boundary

Nations in Two Language Families

Iroquoian	Mohawk Oneida Onondaga Seneca Cayuga Wyandot Huron Tuscarora Cherokee Susquehannock
Muskogean	Alabama Koasati Mikasuki Choctaw Chickasaw Creek

Think About Languages

1. In what part of the present-day United States were the Mikasuki located?

2. What traits do you think the groups in the same language family shared?

Deganawida

longhouse

Deganawida asking a group to join the Iroquois Confederacy ▶

Iroquois Government

When the Iroquois people were a small group, they worked together to solve disagreements. When their numbers began to grow, arguments broke out among clans. According to Iroquois history, two Iroquois leaders, Deganawida and Hiawatha, saw that fighting was destroying their people. In the 1500s, the two leaders urged the Iroquois to work together for peace.

In about 1570, five Iroquois groups joined together to form the **Iroquois Confederacy**, also known as the Iroquois League. Its goal was to maintain peace among the five Iroquois groups, or nations. After the Tuscarora moved to New York from North Carolina in 1722, the Confederacy was called Six Nations. The Confederacy is still active today.

QUICK CHECK

Compare and Contrast **How were the Creek and Iroquois confederacies different?**

Check Understanding

1. **VOCABULARY** Write a sentence using the word about farming from the list below.

   slash-and-burn   wampum
   longhouse   Creek Confederacy

2. **READING SKILL** Compare and Contrast Use your chart from page 40 to write about the people of the Eastern Woodlands.

3. **Write About It** How did Native Americans farm in the forests of the Eastern Woodlands?

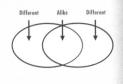

45

Vocabulary

Number a paper from 1 to 4. Beside each number, write the word from the list below that matches the description.

potlatch   travois

migrate   slash-and-burn

1. A sled-like device used to transport goods
2. A method of clearing land for farming
3. To move from one place to another
4. A special feast at which the guests receive gifts

Comprehension and Critical Thinking

5. How did the geography of the Tlingit region help them trade with other groups?
6. **Reading Skill** How was the Creek Confederacy different from the Iroquois Confederacy?
7. **Critical Thinking** How did the environment of the Southwest affect the groups that lived there?
8. **Critical Thinking** In what way did trade help Native Americans?

Skill

Use Parallel Time Lines

Write a complete sentence to answer each question.

9. Which culture developed first, the Hohokam or Ancestral Pueblo?
10. Which two events happened at the same time on the time line?

Hohokam Events

circa 300
Hohokam culture begins

circa 1100
Peak of Hohokam culture

circa 1500
Hohokam culture ends

300   600   900   1200   1500

circa 700
Ancestral Pueblo culture begins

circa 1100
Peak of Ancestral Pueblo culture

circa 1300
Ancestral Pueblo culture ends

Ancestral Pueblo Events

Illinois Standards Achievement Test Preparation

Native American culture is determined by the environment. The Arctic is extremely cold. By contrast, the dry deserts of southern California are very hot. Native American cultures in these areas adapted to the climate and natural resources of the surroundings.

The Inuit in Alaska found ways to live during the bitterly cold Arctic winters. On hunting trips, men built igloos, temporary shelters, of snow blocks. During warm weather, hunters made tents from wooden poles and animal skins. The Inuit hunted walruses, seals, and fish.

1

Paragraph 2 of this passage is mainly about—

Ⓐ how the Arctic is very cold.
Ⓑ how the Inuit survived.
Ⓒ native American culture.
Ⓓ the deserts of California.

2

Read the sentence: "Each culture adapted to the climate and natural resources of their surroundings."
Which of the following words is a synonym for the word *surroundings* as used in the above sentence?

Ⓐ Environment
Ⓑ Life
Ⓒ Change
Ⓓ Feelings

3

What word in the first paragraph tells you that two things are being compared?

Ⓐ Determines
Ⓑ Adapted
Ⓒ Surroundings
Ⓓ Contrast

4

To learn more about the Inuit, the reader should ask—

Ⓐ how Native Americans adapted to deserts in southern California.
Ⓑ what materials the Inuit used to build their homes.
Ⓒ what kinds of tools the Inuit used to hunt.
Ⓓ what is the climate of the eastern woodlands.

The Big Idea Activities

How do people adapt to where they live?

Write About the Big Idea

Descriptive Essay
Use the Unit 1 Foldable to help you write a descriptive essay that answers the Big Idea question, *How do people adapt to where they live?* Be sure to begin your essay with an introduction. Use the notes you wrote under each tab in the Foldable for details to support each main idea. Be sure to describe how the group's location affected its way of life.

FOLDABLES™
Study Organizer

Hunter-Gatherers

Farming Cultures

Make a Model Shelter

Make a model of one of the Native American shelters you read about in the unit.

1. Choose a shelter that you would like to live in.

2. Use your textbook and additional research to choose the best materials to construct your shelter.

3. You may choose to make only the exterior of the shelter or a diorama of the interior.

When you have finished your model, write a paragraph describing why you would like to live in the shelter. Include facts and a description about the shelter you have created.

Unit 2

EXPLORE
The
Big
Idea

Essential Question
What happens when
different cultures first meet?

FOLDABLES
Study Organizer

Cause and Effect
Make and label a
Concept Map Foldable
book before you read this
unit. Across the top write **When
different cultures meet.** Label the
three tabs **Before, During,** and
After. Use the Foldable to organize
information as you read.

When different
cultures meet

Before	During	After

**LOG
ON**

For more about Unit 2 go to
www.macmillanmh.com

The *Niña,* the *Pinta,* and the *Santa
María* set sail on the Atlantic Ocean.

Exploration and
Colonization

PEOPLE, PLACES, AND EVENTS

Marco Polo

Silk Road

1295 | Marco Polo describes China

Christopher Columbus

San Salvador

1492 | Columbus lands on San Salvador

1250   1350   1450

In 1295 **Marco Polo** returned to Venice and described China for the first time to amazed Europeans.

Today you can visit cities that were once major trading posts along the **Silk Road**.

In 1492 **Christopher Columbus** landed in North America, but he thought he had reached Asia!

Today a stone monument on **San Salvador** marks the place where Columbus landed.

Moctezuma II

Tenochtitlán

1502 | Moctezuma II comes to power in Tenochtitlán

Massasoit

Massachusetts

1621 | Wampanoag and Pilgrims celebrate Thanksgiving

1550   1650   1750

Moctezuma II ruled the Aztec from **Tenochtitlán**, a city of more than 200,000 people.

Today Mexico City, Mexico, is built on the site of Tenochtitlán.

In 1621 **Massasoit** and other Wampanoag joined the Pilgrims at Plymouth Plantation for a **Thanksgiving** celebration.

Today you can celebrate Thanksgiving at a modern-day Plymouth Plantation.

Lesson 1

VOCABULARY

profit p. 54

barter p. 54

merchant p. 54

navigation p. 57

READING SKILL

Cause and Effect

Copy the chart below. As you read, fill in information about the European exploration of Asia and North America.

Cause	→	Effect
	→	
	→	
	→	

Illinois Learning Standards

16.A.2b, 16.A.2c, 17.C.2c, 17.D.2a, 18.C.2

THE WORLD Expands

Vikings were the first explorers from Europe to reach North America.

Visual Preview

How did events in Europe affect exploration?

A Vikings sailed along Europe's coasts and rivers and reached North America.

B Europeans learned about Asian inventions from travelers and traders.

C New navigation tools opened trade to Africa and Asia.

D Bartolomeu Dias and Vasco da Gama sailed to Asia for trade.

A THE MIDDLE AGES

About 1,500 years ago, Europe was divided into small kingdoms that were often at war. Most people were poor farmers who rarely left the villages where they were born. Their worlds were very small.

During the Middle Ages, few Europeans knew anything about Asia or Africa—or even about nearby kingdoms. The Middle Ages are a period of European history that ranges from A.D. 500 to 1500. It came between the end of ancient Rome and the beginning of the age of exploration.

Northern Traders and Raiders

The first people of the Middle Ages to travel to distant regions were the Norse, or "north people," who lived in what are today Denmark, Sweden, and Norway. They were skilled sailors who traveled through Europe by ocean and rivers. Their ships carried furs, fish, and timber. The Norse traded those items for oil, spices, and goods from Europe and western Asia.

Norse sailors often acted more like pirates than traders. They are also called Vikings, from the Norse word for "raiders." Viking raids terrified the people of Europe for centuries.

Around A.D. 1000, Viking explorers became the first Europeans to reach North America. They sailed west and built settlements in Iceland and Greenland. Historians believe that disease and battles with native peoples caused settlers to abandon the settlements. As a result, the Viking exploration of North America remained unknown for centuries.

QUICK CHECK

Cause and Effect **Why were the Norse also known as Vikings?**

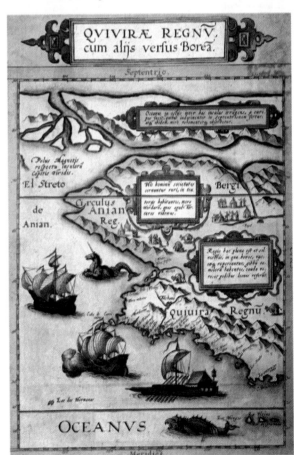

▲ Old maps showed sea monsters in unknown ocean regions.

53

B TRADE AND TRAVEL

During the Middle Ages, travel was dangerous and difficult. Most roads were only muddy paths. Yet some Europeans crossed the continent and traveled east on foot, on horseback, or on sailing vessels.

The Crusades

In 1095 thousands of Europeans prepared for a long journey to Jerusalem in western Asia. The city had great religious importance to Jews, Christians, and Muslims.

In 1096 the first of many wars for control of Jerusalem began. European Christians hoped to capture Jerusalem from the Muslim Turks who ruled it. These wars were known by those in Europe as the Crusades. The Crusaders captured Jerusalem, but wars for control of the city continued for centuries.

Trade and Merchants

The Crusades gave Europeans greater contact with Asia. Many Europeans who joined the Crusades returned with items that were unknown in Europe, such as silk or spices. These returning travelers found that Europeans were willing to pay a lot for items such as cotton, pepper, and cinnamon. They became traders who made a **profit** by charging more than they paid for products. Profit is the money that remains after the costs of running a business.

Soon, a new class of people formed called **merchants**. Merchants made their living from buying and selling goods. Some merchants exchanged goods for other goods, rather than for money. This system is called **barter**.

The Travels of Marco Polo

In 1295 a family of merchants named Polo returned to Venice after many years away. They had traveled thousands of miles across Asia, visiting places no European had ever seen. They had lived as guests in the palace of the ruler of China. One member of the family, Marco Polo, had left at 17 years old and was 43 when he returned.

In China, the Polos saw items unknown in Europe, including paper money and gunpowder. They ate foods that were unknown in Europe, such as noodles. Back in Venice, Marco Polo described the wonders he had seen. A writer named Rustichello wrote down his stories in a book known today as *The Travels of Marco Polo*. The book's description of the world beyond Europe inspired many Europeans to look for new routes to Asia.

PLACES

The city of **Venice** is built on small islands in northeast Italy. In Marco Polo's time, the city was a center for trade between Europe and western Asia. At that time, it was the wealthiest city in Europe.

Venice

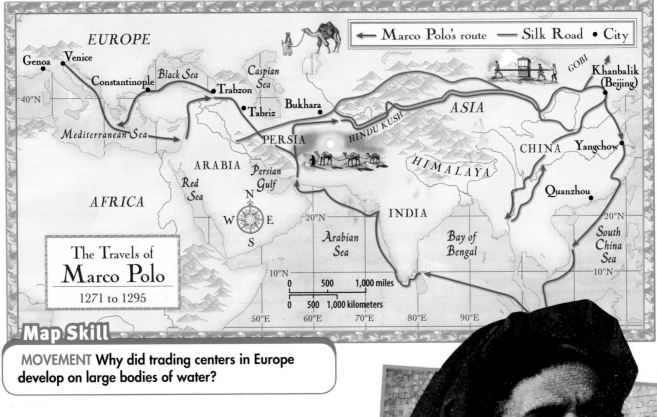

Marco Polo's route — Silk Road • City

The Travels of Marco Polo
1271 to 1295

Map Skill

MOVEMENT **Why did trading centers in Europe develop on large bodies of water?**

Trade with Asia

From about A.D. 100 until the 1300s, Chinese traders brought silk to western Asia. From there it was brought to Europe by merchants. The traders traveled on a famous route called the Silk Road, which connected Asia and Europe. Besides silk, the traders brought spices and jewels along this route.

Traveling between Europe and Asia was difficult. European merchants first had to travel by boat to reach western Asia. Then they traveled by land across the deserts of central Asia. It was a dangerous journey that could take years. If someone could find a new route to Asia, it would save time and money.

▲ Marco Polo became famous for the stories of his travels across Asia and his years living in China.

QUICK CHECK

Cause and Effect **How did the arrival of silk and spices from Asia help the merchant class to arise?**

ⓒ NEW TRADE ROUTES

Europe and Asia were not the only important centers of trade in the 1400s. Africa was also an important trading center. Many parts of Africa were rich in natural resouces. Salt from North Africa was bartered for gold from West African kingdoms. At that time, salt was as valuable as gold because it kept meat from spoiling. The wealth of African kingdoms drew traders from western Asia who were Muslims.

African Kingdoms

As more Muslim traders came to West Africa, many West Africans became followers of Islam. Trade links were formed with merchants in Arabia. In the 1350s, the ruler of a kingdom called Mali traveled to the Muslim holy city of Mecca in Arabia. Along the way, the ruler gave away so much gold that the metal lost its value for ten years. Another African kingdom, Songhai, was larger than all of Europe in the 1400s.

African kingdoms fought among themselves in the 1400s. War weakened most kingdoms. Then, the discovery of gold in the Americas ended African control of Europe's gold supply. Europeans began to enslave Africans in the 1500s, and the great kingdoms collapsed.

A School for Sailors

In the 1400s, Portugal was a small country on the Atlantic coast of western Europe. It was far from Asia, but close to Africa. At that time, land routes to Asia were controlled by Portugal's enemies. Prince Henry of Portugal believed that ships could sail south along the western coast of Africa to reach Asia.

European explorers had not followed this route before. Prince Henry was eager to gain a share of Asia's wealth for Portugal. He also believed that trade with African kingdoms would grow if new sea routes were followed.

▲ Chinese compasses

LAPIS POLARIS MAGNES

▲ An important tool in navigation was the astrolabe. It helped sailors measure the height of the sun and the stars above Earth. Sailors used the astrolabe to find their location north or south of the Equator.

▲ Navigators work at Prince Henry's school

Prince Henry invited experts in mapmaking, shipbuilding, and mathematics to his palace. He set up a school where experts worked on problems of **navigation,** finding direction and following routes at sea.

Sailors guessed their latitude north of the Equator by locating the North Star. However, south of the Equator, sailors could no longer see the North Star. The Chinese compass, which pointed north, became an important navigation tool south of the Equator.

Maps were another technology that helped explorers. Mapmaking experts taught Portuguese captains to make maps of the lands they would explore. Later, these maps would be valuable tools because they showed the safest routes to follow along the African coast.

QUICK CHECK

Cause and Effect How did Portugal's location lead the country to explore sea routes to Asia?

D VOYAGES AROUND AFRICA

Portuguese shipbuilders also developed a new ship, the caravel. It had both square and triangle-shaped sails. These sails allowed it to change direction and catch the wind more easily than older ships.

By 1460 Prince Henry's caravels had sailed along more than 2,000 miles of the African coastline. In 1488 Bartolomeu Dias became the first European to sail around the southern tip of Africa, known as the Cape of Good Hope. This brought him to the Indian Ocean.

Dias never reached India. Another Portuguese explorer, Vasco da Gama, sailed across the Indian Ocean and landed at Calicut, India, on May 20, 1498.

QUICK CHECK

Cause and Effect How did the invention of the caravel help Portuguese explorers?

Check Understanding

1. **VOCABULARY** Write one sentence that uses at least two of these words.

   profit   barter

   merchant   navigation

2. **READING SKILL Cause and Effect** Use your chart from page 52 to write a paragraph explaining how the Crusades helped connect Europe and Asia.

3. **Write About It** Write about how trade may have helped to change European attitudes toward other cultures.

◄ Caravels carried explorers over long distances.

Map and Globe Skills

Use Latitude and Longitude Maps

VOCABULARY

global grid
latitude
longitude
absolute location
relative location
parallel
meridian
Prime Meridian

Some maps divide the Earth into a **global grid**, or set of crisscrossing lines. The two sets of lines are called **latitude** and **longitude**. Lines going from east to west are called latitudes. Lines going from north to south are called longitudes. Latitude and longitude are measured in units called degrees. The symbol for degrees is °. The **absolute location** of a place is where latitude and longitude lines cross.

Another way to determine the location of a place is by using **relative location**. Relative location describes where a place or region is located in relation to another. For example, the relative location of the United States is north of Mexico.

Learn It

- A line of latitude is called a **parallel**. Parallels measure distance north and south of the Equator. The Equator is 0° latitude. Lines of latitude north of the Equator are labeled **N.** Those south of the Equator are labeled **S.**

- A line of longitude is called a **meridian**. Meridians measure distance east and west of the **Prime Meridian**. The Prime Meridian is 0° longitude. Meridians that are east of the Prime Meridian are labeled **E.** Meridians west of the Prime Meridian are labeled **W.**

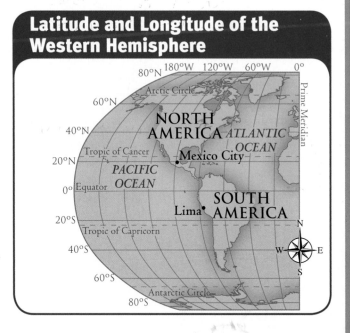

Latitude and Longitude of the Western Hemisphere

Try It

- Locate Mexico City. Which line of latitude is closest to this city?

- Locate Lima in South America. Which line of longitude is closest to this city?

Apply It

- Find the longitude and latitude lines that are closest to your community.

- Which city is closer to your community in longitude, Mexico City or Lima?

SPANIARDS REACH THE AMERICAS

VOCABULARY

expedition p. 61

colony p. 63

Columbian Exchange p. 64

READING SKILL

Cause and Effect

Copy the chart below. As you read, fill in the actions of Spanish explorers and the results.

Cause	→	Effect
	→	
	→	
	→	

Illinois Learning Standards

16.A.2b, 16.A.2c, 17.C.2c, 17.D.2a

Columbus lands in North America.

Visual Preview

How did Spanish explorers change the Americas?

A Queen Isabella paid for Columbus to find a new route to the Indies in 1492.

B Columbus's voyage led to trade with the Taíno people of San Salvador.

C The Columbian Exchange brought new goods to Europe and the Americas.

SAILING WEST TO THE INDIES

European explorers in the 1400s knew the world was large, but they had no idea how large. How could they? Up to this time, they had traveled only to the East.

European explorers were only interested in reaching one place—the Indies. Today we call the region Asia. As you have read, the dream of wealth inspired many explorers to take the risky year-long journey across the Mediterranean Sea, around Africa, and across the Indian Ocean. But one explorer sailed in a different direction. His name was Christopher Columbus.

Queen Isabella

A New Direction

Oceans were the highways of the 1400s. As a result, countries located on the Atlantic Ocean or the Mediterranean Sea became world powers. Two of these powers, Spain and Portugal, were eager to send **expeditions** to the Indies. An expedition is a journey made for a certain purpose such as exploration.

A skilled sailor from Italy named Christopher Columbus approached the rulers of Portugal and Spain with his idea. He wanted to lead an expedition to the Indies—but he wanted to sail in the "wrong" direction. Columbus believed that sailing west for about 3,000 miles would bring him to the Indies. The trip would be faster than the year-long voyage around Africa, he claimed.

Portugal's king wasn't interested in Columbus's idea. The rulers of France and England had no interest either. Finally, Queen Isabella and King Ferdinand of Spain agreed to pay for ships for Columbus. On August 3, 1492, Columbus left Spain with three ships—the *Niña, the Pinta*, and the *Santa María*. Columbus kept two logs, or records, of the voyage. In one log, he recorded the exact distances the ships sailed each day. In the second log, he recorded shorter distances. Some historians believe that Columbus used the second log to mislead other explorers. He wanted to keep his route secret.

QUICK CHECK

Cause and Effect **Why did countries located on oceans become world powers?**

ⓑ REACHING THE AMERICAS

Through August and September of 1492, Columbus's ships sailed across the Atlantic Ocean. Food and water had almost run out when they sighted land on the horizon on October 12.

Today we know that Columbus had reached San Salvador. It is one the Bahama Islands, part of North America. But Columbus believed he had reached the Indies. His crew got a warm welcome from people who paddled out to greet the ships. They carried fresh fruits unlike any the Europeans had ever seen. Columbus called these people "Indios," which is Spanish for "Indians," believing that he had reached his goal. However, the people called themselves the Taíno.

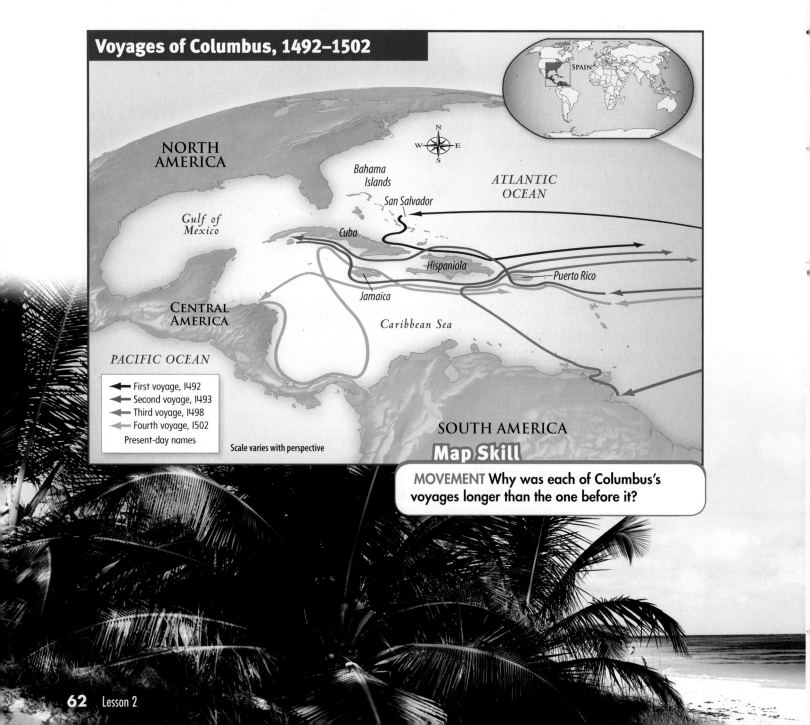

Voyages of Columbus, 1492–1502

SPAIN

NORTH AMERICA

Bahama Islands

San Salvador

ATLANTIC OCEAN

Gulf of Mexico

Cuba

Hispaniola

Puerto Rico

Jamaica

CENTRAL AMERICA

Caribbean Sea

PACIFIC OCEAN

◄— First voyage, 1492
◄— Second voyage, 1493
◄— Third voyage, 1498
◄— Fourth voyage, 1502
Present-day names

Scale varies with perspective

SOUTH AMERICA

Map Skill

MOVEMENT **Why was each of Columbus's voyages longer than the one before it?**

The Taíno

The first meeting between the Spaniards and the Taíno was friendly. The Taíno gave food and gifts to the newcomers to show friendship. In return, Columbus gave the Taíno glass beads and brass bells. Columbus described his gifts as:

> things of small value, in which they took ... pleasure and became so much our friends it was a marvel.
>
> —CHRISTOPHER COLUMBUS

They may have been friends at first, but a century later, disease and violence had destroyed the Taíno. They left no written records. Most of what we know about the Taíno comes from artifacts and Spanish journals. We know that the Taíno cut large canoes from tree trunks. These handmade boats could carry more than 30 people. The Taíno used spears to catch fish. They grew cotton, tobacco, maize, yams, and pineapple. The Taíno also contributed several words to English that you probably know, including hammock and hurricane.

A New Colony

Columbus stayed in what he called the Indies for only a few months. He sailed to other islands in the present-day Caribbean Sea, but he did not find the riches he expected. Taking some Taíno with him, he returned to Spain. When he reported on his expedition, King Ferdinand and Queen Isabella asked Columbus to return to the Caribbean to claim more land.

In 1493 Columbus landed on the island of Hispaniola with more than 1,500 people to set up a Spanish **colony**. A colony is a settlement far from the country that rules it. Today two countries—Haiti and the Dominican Republic—are located on the large island. Columbus made four voyages to the Americas and the Caribbean. On his third voyage, he reached the South American mainland for the first time. He died in 1506, still believing he had reached the Indies.

QUICK CHECK

Cause and Effect How did the arrival of the Spanish change the lives of the Taíno people?

EVENT

Columbus believed he had landed in the Indies. An explorer who followed Columbus claimed that the lands were unknown to Europeans. His name was **Amerigo Vespucci**. On a map made in 1507, a German geographer labeled the land "America," in honor of Vespucci.

Amerigo Vespucci

ACROSS THE ATLANTIC OCEAN

The meeting between the Taíno and Columbus led to what is known today as the **Columbian Exchange**. To exchange means to give something in return for something else. The Columbian Exchange was the movement of people, plants, animals, and diseases across the Atlantic Ocean. It worked out well for Europeans. They were introduced to new foods from the Americas, such as tomatoes and corn. These foods improved the diet of Europeans.

The exchange also introduced food and animals to the Americas. Animals from Europe changed life in America. As you have read, horses changed the way the Native Americans hunted. Cattle and pigs became new food sources. Wool from sheep brought changes to the clothing people wore. Unfortunately,

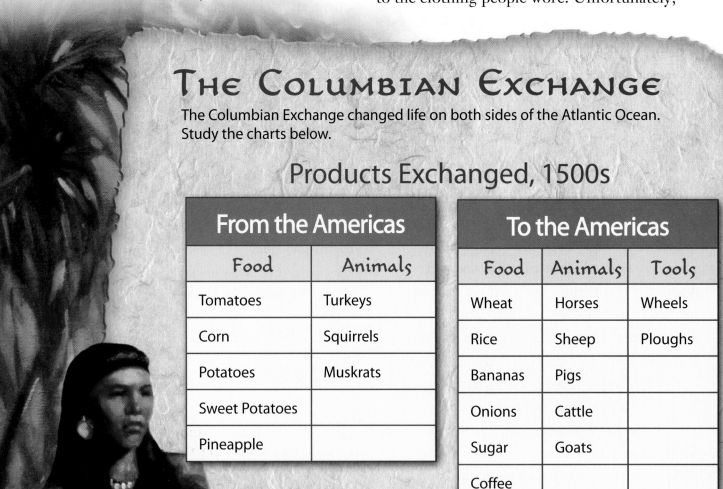

THE COLUMBIAN EXCHANGE

The Columbian Exchange changed life on both sides of the Atlantic Ocean. Study the charts below.

Products Exchanged, 1500s

From the Americas	
Food	Animals
Tomatoes	Turkeys
Corn	Squirrels
Potatoes	Muskrats
Sweet Potatoes	
Pineapple	

To the Americas		
Food	Animals	Tools
Wheat	Horses	Wheels
Rice	Sheep	Ploughs
Bananas	Pigs	
Onions	Cattle	
Sugar	Goats	
Coffee		
Oranges		
Peaches		
Melons		

Europeans and their animals brought germs and diseases that were unknown in the Americas. Smallpox, measles, and other diseases from Europe spread quickly. By 1600, millions of native peoples across the Americas had died.

QUICK CHECK

Cause and Effect How did food from North America change the diet of people in Europe?

Check Understanding

1. **VOCABULARY** Write three sentences about the effects of Columbus's voyages.

   expedition   Columbian Exchange
   colony

2. **READING SKILL Cause and Effect** Use your chart from page 60 to write a paragraph about the effects that animals from Europe had on Native Americans after 1492.

Cause	→	Effect
	→	
	→	
	→	

3. **Write About It** What changes occurred in Europe after Columbus's voyages?

65

VOCABULARY

empire p. 67

conquistador p. 67

READING SKILL

Cause and Effect
Copy the chart below. As you read, fill in the actions of the Spanish and the results.

Cause	→	Effect
	→	
	→	
	→	

Illinois Learning Standards
16.C.2a (W), 17.D.2a, 17.D.2b

Spanish Exploration and Conquest

Tenochtitlán, the Aztec capital, was built on islands in Lake Texcoco. Causeways, or land bridges, led to the mainland.

Visual Preview

How did the arrival of Spanish explorers change Native American empires?

A The Aztec capital fell after attacks by Spaniards and other enemies.

B The Spanish set out to conquer the Inca, the largest empire in South America.

C Spanish soldiers, led by Francisco Pizarro, conquered the Inca Empire.

THE AZTEC EMPIRE

If someone asked you to name the greatest city in the world, what city would you name? If you asked Spanish explorers in 1520, chances are good that many of them would have said that Tenochtitlán was the greatest city in the world.

Tenochtitlán was the capital of the Aztec Empire. An **empire** is a large area in which different groups of people are controlled by one ruler or government.

By 1500 more than 200,000 people lived in Tenochtitlán, making it one of the largest cities in the world. The Aztec controlled about 6 million people.

Cortés Lands in Mexcio

In 1519 the Spaniard Hernan Cortés landed in Mexico with more than 500 **conquistadors**. Conquistador is the Spanish word for conqueror. Several enslaved Africans were among his party. Native people had never seen men with black or white skin. They had never heard guns fired. And they had never seen horses. The Spanish struck fear among the Native people.

Cortés reached Tenochtitlán in November 1519. Moctezuma II, the Aztec ruler, welcomed the Spaniards. But Cortés took Moctezuma prisoner and demanded gold for the king's freedom. The Aztec refused and violence broke out. Moctezuma was killed. Cortés and his men were driven away. But the Spaniards left behind a deadly weapon—smallpox.

Months later, smallpox had killed more than 100,000 Aztec. Cortés returned and destroyed Tenochtitlán. The Spanish capital, Mexico City, was built on the ruins of the Aztec capital.

QUICK CHECK

Cause and Effect Why was Cortés able to return to conquer Tenochtitlán after being driven out?

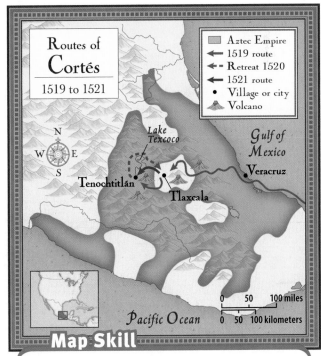

Routes of **Cortés** 1519 to 1521

- Aztec Empire
- ← 1519 route
- ← Retreat 1520
- ← 1521 route
- • Village or city
- ▲ Volcano

Lake Texcoco

Gulf of Mexico

Tenochtitlán

Veracruz

Tlaxcala

Pacific Ocean

0 50 100 miles
0 50 100 kilometers

Map Skill

MOVEMENT Where did Cortés's retreat to in 1521?

67

After the conquest of the Aztec Empire, the Spanish set out to conquer the land to the south. They did not know that another empire—the wealthiest in the world—ruled much of South America. This was the Inca Empire.

At the height of its power, the Inca Empire extended more than 2,500 miles along the western coast of South America. This is about the distance from New York City to Phoenix, Arizona.

Linked by Highways

Most of the Inca Empire was located in the Andes mountain range. The capital of the empire, Cuzco, in present-day Peru, was built at an altitude of 11,000 feet. A system of paved stone roads leading out from Cuzco formed a highway system that tied the empire together. Today Cuzco is one of the highest cities on Earth.

Information was carried along the roads by messengers who were able to run 50 miles a day. They carried knotted strings, called quipus, to help remember information. The Inca used quipus to keep records. String colors stood for objects to be counted. For example, red strings stood for soldiers, and yellow strings measured maize crops. Quipus were an important tool for communicating information, especially as the empire grew larger.

The Inca Empire

ANDES MOUNTAINS

Amazon River

Cajamarca

Cuzco

SOUTH AMERICA

PACIFIC OCEAN

ANDES MOUNTAINS

ATLANTIC OCEAN

N W E S

0   300   600 miles
0   300   600 kilometers

■ Inca Empire
• City

Map Skill

LOCATION **Which city would Spanish explorers most likely enter first? Why?**

Inca Society

Inca society was like European society in some ways. Rulers and religious leaders were the highest class. Instead of paying taxes with money, the Inca provided services, such as repairing roads, digging canals, and building temples for several months each year. Workers received clothing and food for their work. Inca women were required to weave one piece of clothing for the workers each year.

Although the Inca did not use money, gold and silver were important to the society. Gold was called "the sweat of the sun," and silver was called "the tears of the moon." Inca craftworkers made cups, bowls, and plates from these precious metals. These were used mainly by the rulers, nobles, and priests. After the arrival of the Spanish, few of these gold and silver objects remained.

QUICK CHECK

Cause and Effect Why were highways an important part of the Inca Empire's rise to power?

The ruins of Machu Picchu are high in the Andes of Peru.

This painting shows Pizarro, the Spanish conquistador, capturing Atahualpa, the Inca ruler, at the battle of Cajamarca.

C THE FALL OF THE INCA

In 1531 Spanish conquistador Francisco Pizarro landed on the west coast of South America with about 180 men and about 30 horses. At the time Pizarro arrived, the Inca Empire was collapsing. The highway system that allowed messengers to travel easily had allowed disease to spread quickly. Smallpox had entered the empire from Mexico several years earlier. Thousands of Inca people had died, including the Inca ruler, Wayna Capac. After his death, a civil war broke out between his sons, Atahualpa and Huascar, for control of the empire.

Atahualpa controlled the northern part of the empire. He had heard reports about Pizarro's arrival, but he was not worried. Pizarro had only 180 men. The war with Huascar was a more serious problem.

Pizarro reached the Inca town of Cajamarca in 1532. His soldiers knew they were greatly outnumbered by the Inca. One Spanish soldier wrote:

"All were full of fear, for we were so few, and so deep into the land, with no hope of rescue."

Pizarro and Atahualpa

Atahualpa heard reports of Pizarro's arrival. However, Atahualpa didn't send troops against the Spanish. They remained camped outside the city. Atahualpa sent a message to Pizarro, inviting him to meet in the city. Pizarro entered Cajamarca and hid his men around the main square. After the Inca entered the square, Pizarro gave a signal. Guns exploded from doorways and windows. Spaniards on horseback rode into the square, swinging steel swords. Thousands of Atahualpa's men were killed. Pizarro himself took the Inca ruler prisoner.

To earn his freedom, Atahualpa offered to fill a huge room with gold and silver. For months, gold and silver objects arrived from all corners of the empire. But Pizarro was dishonest and refused to release the Inca ruler. When the room was filled, he killed Atahualpa. Then he melted down the precious metal objects into bars of gold and silver to send back to Spain. That's why so few objects remain from the glory days of the Inca Empire—Pizarro turned them into money. By 1540 Spain controlled one of the largest empires in the world.

QUICK CHECK

Cause and Effect How was the Inca Empire weakened before Pizarro arrived?

Check Understanding

1. **VOCABULARY** Write one sentence to show a relationship between the two words below.

   empire   conquistador

2. **READING SKILL Cause and Effect** Use your chart from page 66 to show how the Spanish desire for gold destroyed the Aztec and Inca empires.

Cause	→	Effect
	→	
	→	
	→	

3. **EXPLORE The Big Idea Write About It** How did Spanish exploration change Central and South America?

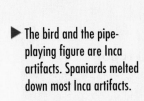

▶ The bird and the pipe-playing figure are Inca artifacts. Spaniards melted down most Inca artifacts.

Lesson 4

VOCABULARY

frontier p. 73

missionary p. 75

enslave p. 75

mestizo p. 76

READING SKILL

Cause and Effect
Copy the chart. As you read, fill it in with causes and effects of Spanish exploration of North America.

Cause	→	Effect
	→	
	→	
	→	

Illinois Learning Standards

15.D.2b, 16.A.2b,
16.C.2a (W), 16.A.2c, 17.D.2b

SPAIN'S OVERSEAS EMPIRE

De Soto explored the Southeast.

Visual Preview

How did Spain's growing empire impact life in North America?

A In the early 1500s, Spaniards explored Florida in search of gold.

B In the 1500s, Spaniards explored the Southwest and expanded colonies.

C Spaniards, Native Americans, and Africans lived in the Spanish colonies.

SPANISH IN NORTH AMERICA

Weighed down by guns and armor, hundreds of men came ashore in blazing heat. In search of gold and adventure, the conquistadors paved the way for Spanish settlers.

For the Spanish, North America was a **frontier** in the 1500s. A frontier is the far edge of a settled area. Modern-day Florida was one early frontier for the Spaniards.

"Place of Flowers"

In 1513 Juan Ponce de León led an expedition in search of a Fountain of Youth that was said to be on an island north of Cuba. He landed near what is today St. Augustine, Florida. He named the land *La Florida*—"place of flowers."

Search for Gold

In 1539 Hernando de Soto landed in Florida with hundreds of men and animals. He explored the present-day southeastern United States. He never found gold. Instead, diseases carried by his men and animals killed thousands of Native Americans.

QUICK CHECK

Cause and Effect How did false stories bring Spanish explorers to Florida?

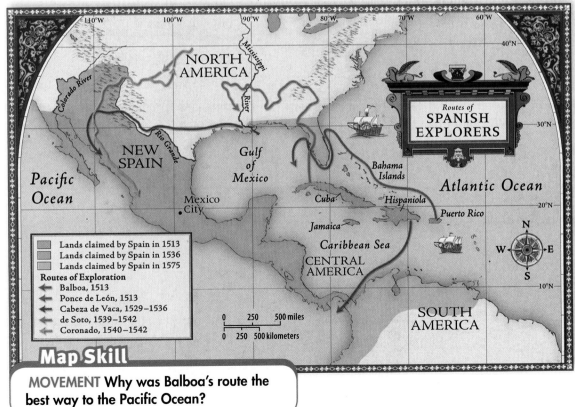

Routes of SPANISH EXPLORERS

NORTH AMERICA

NEW SPAIN

Pacific Ocean

Mexico City

Gulf of Mexico

Cuba

Jamaica

Bahama Islands

Hispaniola

Puerto Rico

Caribbean Sea

CENTRAL AMERICA

Atlantic Ocean

SOUTH AMERICA

Colorado River
Rio Grande
Mississippi River

Lands claimed by Spain in 1513
Lands claimed by Spain in 1536
Lands claimed by Spain in 1575

Routes of Exploration
Balboa, 1513
Ponce de León, 1513
Cabeza de Vaca, 1529–1536
de Soto, 1539–1542
Coronado, 1540–1542

0   250   500 miles
0   250   500 kilometers

Map Skill

MOVEMENT Why was Balboa's route the best way to the Pacific Ocean?

▼ Coronado explored the Southwest.

B NEW SPAIN EXPANDS

Spanish conquistadors continued to explore the frontier in other parts of North America. With each expedition, disease carried by the men and their animals spread quickly among Native Americans.

Explorers in the Southwest

In 1528 Spanish conquistador Álvar Núñez Cabeza de Vaca sailed north from Cuba. A hurricane wrecked his ship on the coast of present-day Texas. Cabeza de Vaca and his men lived in a Native American village for four years. In 1536 they arrived in Mexico City after walking through present-day Texas, New Mexico, and Arizona.

In 1540 Francisco Vásquez de Coronado led an expedition of Spaniards, Africans, and Native Americans across what is now the southwestern United States. He claimed large areas of land for Spain. Coronado and his men were the first Europeans to see the Grand Canyon, located in present-day Arizona.

Colonists Arrive

By 1550 Spain controlled two large territories in the Americas. In South America, the Spanish called the territory Peru. The territory that included Mexico and most of Central America was called New Spain.

As growing numbers of Spaniards settled in New Spain, Spanish rulers took tighter control of the new colony. Rulers gave encomiendas, or large areas of land, to colonists who were loyal to them. The land included many Native American villages. Native Americans were forced to work for the Spanish landowners. On the encomiendas, many Native Americans died from starvation, disease, and overwork.

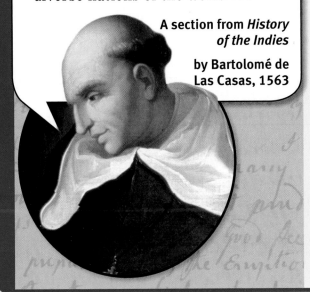

Not only have [Native Americans] shown themselves to be very wise peoples . . . providing for their nations . . . and making them prosper in justice, they have equaled many diverse nations of the world . . .

A section from *History of the Indies*

by Bartolomé de Las Casas, 1563

Write About It Write a letter to de Las Casas explaining what effect his words have on your feelings about Native Americans.

Some colonists spoke out against the treatment of Native Americans. One was Bartolomé de Las Casas. De Las Casas was a **missionary**—a person who tries to persuade people to accept new religious beliefs. De Las Casas's opinions about the Native Americans were different from the opinions of many Spaniards. Read his opinion above.

Africans in New Spain

Spanish explorers brought the first **enslaved** Africans to Mexico. To enslave people is to force them to work against their will. Enslaved Africans were not brought to New Spain in large numbers until many thousands of Native Americans had died. As more encomiendas were settled, more workers were needed.

By 1550, more than 5,000 enslaved Africans were working in the fields of encomiendas in New Spain. Enslaved Africans also worked in the silver mines of New Spain. At the ports of Veracruz and Acapulco, enslaved Africans often loaded silver and other precious metals onto ships bound for Spain.

In the 1570s, some enslaved Africans and Native Americans rebelled. Some rebels were defeated, but others escaped to areas far from the encomiendas where they could be free. After escaping, enslaved Africans and Native Americans built their own communities. These settlements came to be called maroon communities. One leader of a rebellion was an African named Yanga, who had been a king in his homeland. In 1570 Yanga and his followers escaped to the mountains around Veracruz. They built a town called San Lorenzo de los Negros.

▼ A statue of Yanga

QUICK CHECK

Cause and Effect **Why did the growth of encomiendas bring enslaved Africans to Mexico?**

SOCIETY IN NEW SPAIN

New Spain — **Social Pyramid**

Viceroy

Peninsulares

Criollos

Mestizos

Native Americans and Enslaved Africans

Chart Skill

Which groups were at the bottom of the pyramid?

By the middle of the 1500s, three different groups of people—Native Americans, Spanish, and Africans—had created a new society. Its leader was New Spain's ruler, the viceroy. Below him were Spaniards from Spain, called Peninsulares. Below them were people born in New Spain of Spanish parents, called Criollos. Below this group were **mestizos**, people who were both Spanish and Native American. At the bottom of the pyramid were Native Americans and enslaved Africans, forced to work without wages.

From 1600 to 1680, the Spanish built over 20 settlements in New Mexico. These settlements became important centers for missions, where priests tried to convert Native Americans, and for mining natural resources.

In the 1680s the Spanish built settlements in the part of New Spain that is now the state of Texas. They also built settlements along the coast of the Pacific Ocean. By 1800 the Spanish controlled much of what is now Texas, New Mexico, Arizona, and California.

QUICK CHECK

Compare and Contrast How were mestizos different from Spaniards?

Check Understanding

1. **VOCABULARY** Write a short play about the meeting of the two people in the list below. Use the other vocabulary words in the play.

   frontier   enslave
   missionary   mestizo

2. **READING SKILL Cause and Effect** Use the cause and effect chart on page 72 to help you write a paragraph about the change that occurred after the Spanish explored North America.

Cause	→	Effect
	→	
	→	
	→	

3. **Write About It** What do you think happened when the Native Americans and Spanish settlers met for the first time?

Chart and Graph Skills

Compare Line and Circle Graphs

VOCABULARY

line graph
circle graph

When European explorers arrived in the Americas, both Native American and European cultures experienced change. One way you can measure changes is to use **line graphs** and **circle graphs**. A line graph shows a change over time. A circle graph shows how something can be divided into parts. All of the parts together make up a circle. Circle graphs are also called pie graphs because the parts look like slices of pie.

Learn It

- To find out what information a graph contains, look at its title.

- Study the labels on a graph. Labels on a line graph appear along the bottom of the graph and along the left side. Labels on a circle graph explain the subject.

Try It

- Look at the line graph. What was the Taíno population of Hispaniola in 1570?

- Look at the circle graph. Which group made up the largest part of the population of Hispaniola in 1570?

Apply It

- Summarize the line graph's information about the Taíno people on Hispaniola.

- Summarize the circle graph's information about the people of Hispaniola in 1570.

- Summarize what both graphs tell you about the meeting of different cultures.

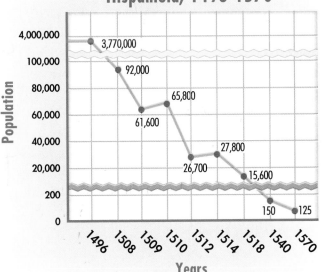

Taíno Population of Hispaniola, 1496-1570

Population / Years

4,000,000 — 3,770,000
100,000 — 92,000
80,000 — 65,800
60,000 — 61,600
40,000
27,800
20,000 — 26,700
15,600
200
150 125
0

1496 1508 1509 1510 1512 1514 1518 1540 1570

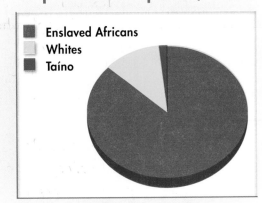

Population of Hispaniola, 1570

- Enslaved Africans
- Whites
- Taíno

VOCABULARY

Northwest Passage
p. 79

merchant company
p. 80

READING SKILL

Cause and Effect
Copy the cause and effect chart below. As you read, list the causes and effects of the search for the Northwest Passage.

Cause	→	Effect
	→	
	→	
	→	

Illinois Learning Standards
17.A.2a, 17.D.2b

SEARCHING FOR THE NORTHWEST PASSAGE

Dutch ships such as these brought explorers to the Americas and Asia.

Visual Preview

How did the search for the Northwest Passage affect people?

A Europeans learned about North America while exploring the east coast.

B Henry Hudson explored the Hudson River and traded with the Lenni Lenape.

A EUROPEANS SAIL WEST

Trade with Asia brought huge profits for European countries that were trading silk, spices, and other goods. Sailing east around Africa, however, took months. Was there a quicker way to reach Asia?

In the 1490s and 1500s, many Europeans believed there was a water route across North America. They believed this route connected the Atlantic to the Pacific Ocean. This shortcut, which no one was sure existed, was called the **Northwest Passage**.

Explorations in North America

You have read how ships had to sail around Africa to reach Asia. European rulers thought that finding a Northwest Passage would help them reach Asia in much less time than the African route. In 1497 the king of England hired an Italian, John Cabot, to find this shorter route to Asia. Cabot sailed west and sighted land at Newfoundland, an island off the coast of Canada.

Cabot did not find a Northwest Passage, but he came upon something valuable. He found an area of the Atlantic Ocean southeast of Newfoundland. These waters were so crowded with fish that sailors scooped them into baskets dropped over the sides of their ships. Soon, some colonists would make a lot of money shipping dried fish to Europe.

In 1524 France hired an Italian explorer named Giovanni da Verrazano to continue the search for a Northwest Passage. Verrazano explored the east coast of North America. He reached the New York Harbor and the mouth of what would later be called the Hudson River. Even though he didn't find the Northwest Passage, Verrazano discovered one of the most important rivers in North America.

QUICK CHECK

Cause and Effect **What effect did Cabot's voyage have on Europeans?**

Giovanni da Verrazano ▶

THE SEARCH GOES ON

All of Europe was abuzz with talk of a Northwest Passage. Merchants realized that if the Northwest Passage were found, they could make huge profits. Dutch merchants began to lead the way.

A New Kind of Company

In 1602 Dutch merchants founded the first **merchant company**. This company was a group of business people who shared the costs of a trading voyage. They would also share the profits from the spices brought back from Asia. The question was, would they see a profit? It was a huge risk.

One merchant company that was willing to take the risk was the Dutch East India Company. In 1609 it hired an English sea captain, Henry Hudson, to find a shortcut to Asia. Hudson believed that North America was only about 70 miles wide. He also believed that the Northwest Passage was located north of Virginia. He sailed along the Atlantic coast of North America. In August Hudson explored Chesapeake and Delaware Bays. Neither of these waterways was the Northwest Passage.

▲ Henry Hudson

When Hudson reached New York Harbor, he mapped it and traded with the local Native Americans, the Lenni Lenape. But the relationship between the Dutch and the Lenni Lenape was not always peaceful. Hudson's crew wrote of battles.

Hudson sailed about 150 miles north on the river that flowed into the harbor, thinking he had found the Northwest Passage. He soon discovered that it contained freshwater. Hudson's reports of rich soil and resources would encourage the Dutch to start a colony there.

Exploring Hudson Bay

On Hudson's second voyage in 1610, he explored what is now Hudson Bay while searching for the Northwest Passage. As winter set in, his ship, the *Discovery*, froze in the ice. When spring came, Hudson tried to continue his voyage. By this time, his crew was tired of the harsh conditions aboard ship. They had been living on moldy bread and rotten meat. The threat of mutiny, or naval revolt, filled the air. The crew did not kill Hudson, but they

The Hudson River ▼

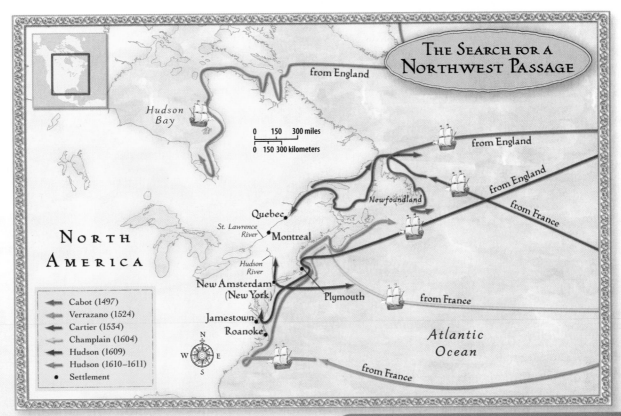

THE SEARCH FOR A
NORTHWEST PASSAGE

from England

Hudson
Bay

0 150 300 miles
0 150 300 kilometers

from England

from England

from France

Newfoundland

NORTH
AMERICA

Quebec

St. Lawrence
River
Montreal

Hudson
River

New Amsterdam
(New York)

Plymouth

from France

Jamestown
Roanoke

Atlantic
Ocean

N
W   E
S

→ Cabot (1497)
→ Verrazano (1524)
→ Cartier (1534)
→ Champlain (1604)
→ Hudson (1609)
→ Hudson (1610–1611)
• Settlement

from France

Map Skill

MOVEMENT About how many miles of coastline did Verrazano explore?

did take over the ship. Hudson, his son, and eight loyal sailors were placed into a small boat. They were never seen again. When the *Discovery* reached England, its crew was arrested.

QUICK CHECK

Cause and Effect What was the result of Hudson's search for the Northwest Passage?

Check Understanding

1. **VOCABULARY** Write one sentence using both of these vocabulary terms.

   Northwest Passage
   merchant company

2. **READING SKILL Cause and Effect** Use your cause and effect chart from page 78 to write about the Northwest Passage.

Cause	→	Effect
	→	
	→	
	→	

3. **Write About It** Why do you think there were battles between Native Americans and Hudson's crew?

VOCABULARY

ally p. 83

coureurs de bois p. 84

import p. 84

export p. 84

voyageur p. 84

READING SKILL

Cause and Effect

Copy the chart below. As you read, list the causes and effects of the fur trade in New France.

Cause	→	Effect
	→	
	→	
	→	

Illinois Learning Standards

16.B.2a (US), 17.D.2b

THE FIRST FRENCH COLONIES

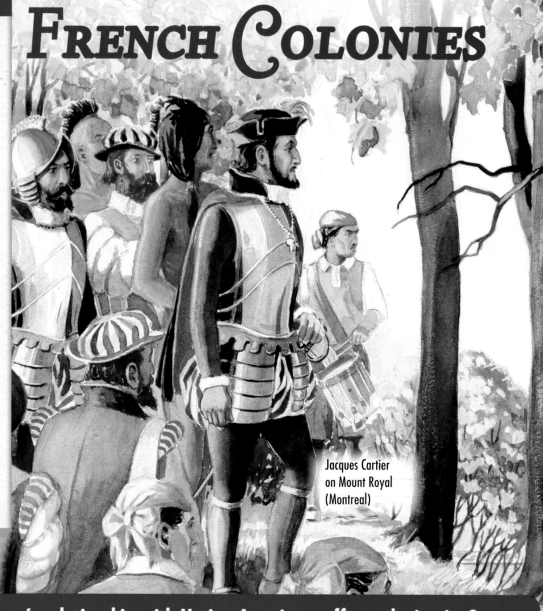

Jacques Cartier on Mount Royal (Montreal)

Visual Preview

How did France's relationship with Native Americans affect colonization?

A The French traded fur with Native Americans living around French settlements.

B New France attracted fur hunters, missionaries, and explorers.

Even though Verazzano failed to find the Northwest Passage, France continued to look for the route. In 1534 Jacques Cartier reached a peninsula near the St. Lawrence River and claimed it for France.

After three voyages in which he failed to find the Northwest Passage, Cartier returned to France disappointed. Except for a few French companies that traded with Native Americans for furs, France paid little attention to the colony for nearly 60 years.

Founding of Quebec

Starting in 1598, France tried to establish a permanent settlement called New France. It hoped that the settlement would expand the fur trade and make money for France. These attempts failed. Then, in 1608, King Henry IV sent Samuel de Champlain to New France as its governor. Champlain established a fur trading post at Quebec.

Fur coats and hats were very popular in Europe at the time. Champlain knew that if he managed the colony well, he could make a lot of money in the fur trade. In order to strengthen the colony, he established friendly relations with several Native American groups. Soon the French, Wyandot, and Algonquin became **allies**, or political and military partners. With French firearms, these Native American groups easily defeated their longtime enemy, the Iroquois.

QUICK CHECK

Cause and Effect Why did France want to establish a permanent settlement in New France?

▲ Samuel de Champlain's arrival at Quebec

Many young French men were eager to make money from the fur trade. They became hunters and trappers called **coureurs de bois**, or "runners of the woods." So many hunters came to New France that Europe's **imports** of furs soared. Import means to bring in goods from another country for sale or use. **Export** means to send goods to another country. French officials feared the fur imports would oversupply the market and bring the price of fur down. To control the price of fur, the French government issued permits to trappers, hoping to limit their number. Those who received permits were called **voyageurs**.

New France's Slow Growth

In the early 1600s, King Louis XIII began to expand New France. He allowed more people to settle there, but few French colonists came. One reason was that the king preferred Roman Catholics to settle the colony. French people who were not Catholic were more likely to settle in the English colonies of North America. In 1666 only 3,215 colonists lived in New France.

Louis XIII also sent Catholic missionaries to Canada. French missionaries often lived among the Native Americans as they tried to convert them. Missionaries built churches at trading centers.

The Search for a Passage Continues

Meanwhile, the French continued to search for the Northwest Passage. When Champlain returned to New France in 1610, he brought along seventeen-year-old Étienne Brûlé. The young man was eager to explore. Years earlier Champlain had searched for the Northwest Passage. This time he sent Brûlé to look for it.

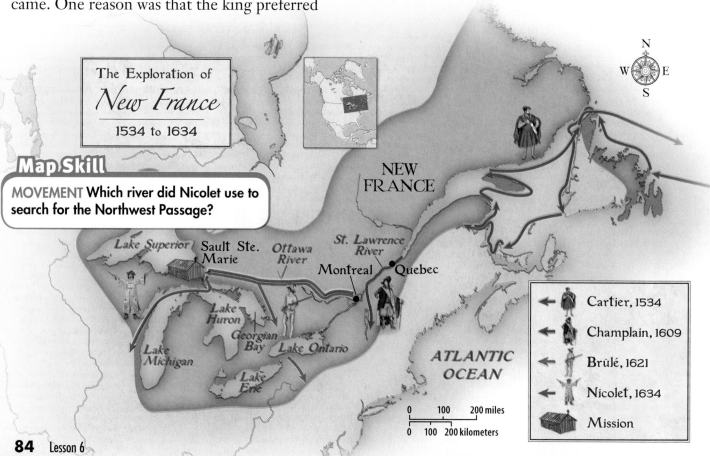

The Exploration of
New France
1534 to 1634

Map Skill

MOVEMENT **Which river did Nicolet use to search for the Northwest Passage?**

NEW FRANCE

Lake Superior Sault Ste. Marie Ottawa River St. Lawrence River Montreal Quebec

Lake Huron Georgian Bay Lake Ontario

Lake Michigan Lake Erie

ATLANTIC OCEAN

← Cartier, 1534
← Champlain, 1609
← Brûlé, 1621
← Nicolet, 1634
Mission

0   100   200 miles
0   100   200 kilometers

Samuel de Champlain sailing up the St. Lawrence River in 1603

Young Brûlé was the first French explorer to see Lake Huron. He explored the western edge of Lake Huron, then turned back. During his search for the Northwest Passage, Brûlé also explored parts of Lake Ontario, Lake Erie, and Lake Superior. By the end of his career, he had explored four of the Great Lakes.

In 1617 another explorer, Jean Nicolet, continued the search for the Northwest Passage. Nicolet followed the route that Étienne Brûlé took to Lake Huron. Then he pushed on and went further than Brûlé. He became the first European to see Lake Michigan. Both Brûlé and Nicolet lived amongst Native American groups and explored the Great Lakes region.

QUICK CHECK

Cause and Effect Why did New France fail to grow?

Check Understanding

1. **VOCABULARY** Write about fur trappers using these vocabulary terms.

   coureurs de bois   voyageurs

2. **READING SKILL Cause and Effect** Use your cause and effect chart from page 82 to write about the fur trade in New France.

Cause	→	Effect
	→	
	→	
	→	

3. **Write About It** Write about why the Wyandot, Algonquin, and French became allies.

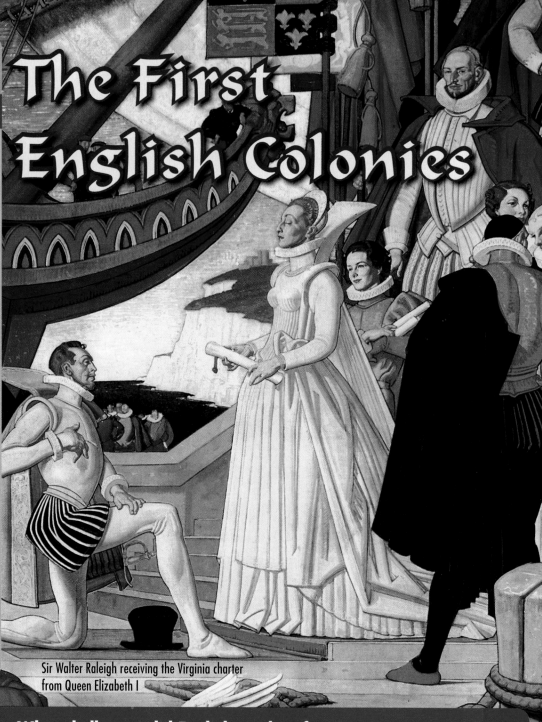

The First English Colonies

Lesson 7

VOCABULARY

charter p. 87

cash crop p. 88

indentured servant p. 89

House of Burgesses p. 89

Pilgrim p. 90

sachem p. 92

READING SKILL

Cause and Effect

Copy the chart below. As you read, list the causes and effects of the Pilgrims settling in Plymouth.

Cause	→	Effect
	→	
	→	
	→	

Illinois Learning Standards

16.B.2a (US), 17.D.2b

Sir Walter Raleigh receiving the Virginia charter from Queen Elizabeth I

Visual Preview

What challenges did English settlers face?

A Both attempts to settle Roanoke Island were failures.

B Colonists at Jamestown had trouble making a profit until they grew tobacco.

C Pilgrims created a plan of self-government called the Mayflower Compact.

D The Pilgrims had trouble growing food, but were helped by the Wampanoag.

A THE LOST COLONY

While Spain was getting rich from its colonies in the Americas, England's Queen Elizabeth I and her adviser, Sir Walter Raleigh, came up with a plan to make England a power in the Americas.

In 1585 Queen Elizabeth gave Sir Walter Raleigh a **charter**. A charter is an official document that grants its holder special rights. The charter said that Raleigh was supposed to start a colony for the purpose of finding gold and other riches in North America. Raleigh called the new colony Virginia. Virginia was named in honor of Queen Elizabeth I, the Virgin, or unmarried, Queen.

Raleigh's First Try

After sending explorers to find a good place for a colony, Sir Walter Raleigh decided upon what is now Roanoke, North Carolina. About 100 men were sent to Roanoke Island. Many of the colonists had little experience living off the land. They did not know what supplies they would need. Instead of planting crops, the colonists traded with several Native American groups for food. When Native American groups were not interested in the trade, some colonists stole food. As a result, fighting broke out. Meanwhile, the colonists did not find gold. After a difficult winter, the colonists returned to England.

Raleigh Tries Again

In 1587 John White and a second group of colonists settled in Virginia. Supplies ran low and White returned to England for help. He arrived just as war between England and Spain broke out, and England needed all its ships. White did not return until 1590. When he arrived, the colony was empty. No one knows what happened to the colonists.

QUICK CHECK

Cause and Effect **Why were the Roanoke settlements failures?**

A reconstruction of the ship that brought colonists to Roanoke Island ▶

Captain John Smith

▲ Today you can visit a model of colonial Jamestown to see how the settlers lived.

ⓑ THE JAMESTOWN COLONY

The English decided to continue searching for gold in North America. King James I gave a charter to a merchant company called the Virginia Company. In 1607 the Virginia Company sent a group of 144 men and boys to start a new settlement. The colonists landed near a river that they named the James River. They built a new settlement there called Jamestown. It was the first permanent English settlement in North America.

Captain John Smith

Like the Roanoke colony, the Jamestown colony soon ran out of food. It survived only because of the leadership of John Smith, who proclaimed, "Those who don't work, don't eat!" Smith forced the colonists to plant crops and build homes. In 1609 Smith was injured when his gunpowder bag exploded, and he returned to England. Without him, the colonists stopped working. The winter after Smith left was called "the starving time." By the end of the winter, only 60 of the settlers were alive.

A New Crop

The Jamestown colonists discovered that Virginia had the perfect soil and climate for growing tobacco. Tobacco had been recently introduced into Europe, and the demand for it was growing.

Colonist John Rolfe harvested the first tobacco crop, which was a huge success. Tobacco became Virginia's first **cash crop**, or crop grown to be sold for profit. Soon the demand for tobacco was so great that new fields were needed. The colonists decided to take land that belonged to the Powhatan, a group of nearby Native Americans.

Growing tobacco required many field workers. To attract workers, the Virginia Company paid travel expenses from Europe for people who would work in tobacco fields. These **indentured servants** promised to pay back the travel expenses by working five to seven years. After their time of service, they received land and supplies to start farms.

Jamestown's First Government

People in England had been electing their governments for a long time. The Virginia Company, therefore, allowed colonists to establish a colonial assembly similar to the one in England. The representatives were known as burgesses. The assembly, called the **House of Burgesses**, made laws for the colony. Only white men who owned land could vote for representatives. The House of Burgesses first met July 30, 1619, making it the first elected assembly of Europeans in the Americas.

The Powhatan Fight Back

As Jamestown grew, the colonists took more and more land. This threatened the Powhatan way of life. In 1622 the Powhatan attacked English villages. Nearly 350 English settlers, about one-third of the colonists, were killed. These attacks convinced King James I to cancel the Virginia Company charter. In 1624 the colony became a royal colony under the direct control of the king.

PEOPLE

The Powhatan were a strong and united group. **Pocahontas**, the daughter of the Powhatan chief, often visited Jamestown. In 1614 John Rolfe married Pocahontas. Their marriage helped keep peace between the Powhatan and the colonists. The "Peace of Pocahontas" lasted for several years.

Pocahontas

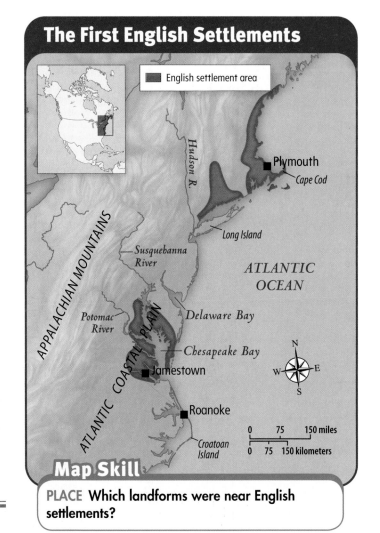

The First English Settlements

English settlement area

Map Skill

PLACE Which landforms were near English settlements?

QUICK CHECK

Cause and Effect **Why was Jamestown a successful colony?**

By 1534 King Henry VIII had left the Roman Catholic Church and established the Church of England. In the early 1600s, some groups in England wanted to leave the Church of England. People called Separatists wanted to separate and form their own churches. This type of action was not allowed in England.

Many Separatists were threatened by the English government and tossed into jails. This led one group of Separatists, known as **Pilgrims**, to ask permission to settle in Virginia. A pilgrim is someone who travels to a place for religious reasons. The Virginia Company agreed to pay for the voyage.

The Mayflower

On September 16, 1620, the Pilgrims and other colonists boarded the *Mayflower* at Plymouth, England, and set sail for Virginia. On board were more than 100 men, women, and children. For 66 days the tiny, crowded ship crossed the Atlantic Ocean. Finally, in November someone spotted land.

The *Mayflower* had reached land, but not Virginia. The Pilgrims came ashore on Cape Cod in what is now Massachusetts. By the time they landed, it was almost winter. They decided to settle the area near where they landed. The Pilgrims called their settlement New Plymouth, which is today Plymouth, Massachusetts.

A Step Toward Self-Government

The Pilgrims took steps to establish a new colony in this place not yet claimed by England. Before they left the ship, the Pilgrims wrote a form of government for their new colony. They called their agreement the Mayflower Compact. The compact, or agreement, was an early plan of self-government by colonists in North America. Only men signed the compact.

◀ The *Mayflower* often sailed in rough seas as it crossed the Atlantic Ocean.

Life in Plymouth

The Pilgrims had a difficult time almost from the beginning. By the time they landed, it was cold, making it more difficult to build a colony. The Pilgrims did manage to build some small shelters, but many avoided the frigid cold by huddling together on the *Mayflower*.

Some of the Plymouth colonists were from cities such as London, and had never farmed. In addition, the Pilgrims were not prepared for harsh Massachusetts winters. By the end of the first winter, almost half of the 100 settlers had died from starvation and disease. If it had not been for the help of nearby Native Americans, all of the settlers might have died.

QUICK CHECK

Cause and Effect **Why did many Pilgrims die during the first winter?**

Citizenship

Cooperation and Compromise

People cooperate when they work together to make rules or laws or to solve a problem. People compromise when they give up part of something they want. By getting along and working together, everyone contributes to a solution.

Write About It Write a paragraph about a time you gave up something you wanted in order to solve a problem or settle a disagreement.

◀ These reenactors show Pilgrim life after the first difficult year.

NATIVE AMERICANS SAVE THE DAY

Remember all those people searching for the Northwest Passage? By the time the Pilgrims arrived, disease carried by Europeans had killed many of the Native Americans in the region. One of the largest groups, the Wampanoag, had lived for centuries along the coast where the Pilgrims landed. The Massachuset, Narragansett, Pequot, and Mohegan groups also lived in the area.

Helping the Pilgrims

Massasoit was the Wampanoag **sachem**. A sachem, or leader, was the head of each group of Native Americans. One person living among the Wampanoag was a member of the Pawtuxet named Squanto. In 1615 he had been captured by English sailors and eventually learned to speak English. A sachem called Samoset learned to speak English from fishermen who visited the area. These three Native Americans helped the Pilgrims survive their first years in the region we call New England.

The Pilgrims had settled on land that was once the home of the Pawtuxet. Disease had wiped out the Pawtuxet years earlier. Squanto decided to live among the Pilgrims and farm

his Pawtuxet land. He showed the Pilgrims how to grow maize, using fish to fertilize the soil. He taught the newcomers how to trap rabbits, deer, and other wild animals. He also showed them where to fish.

Thanksgiving

By the fall of 1621, the Pilgrims had built seven houses in the Plymouth colony. With the help of Squanto, they learned to grow maize and barley. The Pilgrims celebrated their first harvest with three days of feasting. Massasoit and 90 Wampanoag came to the feast, bringing five deer. The Pilgrims added wild goose and duck.

▼ This recreation of Thanksgiving brought together descendants of Pilgrims and Native Americans who took part in the first Plymouth Thanksgiving.

During this time many Native American and European groups held harvest festivals to give thanks for the growth of their crops. The Spanish, French, and English colonists held thanksgiving services in America before the Pilgrims' celebration in 1621. The feast shared by the Pilgrims and Wampanoag would later be called our country's first "thanksgiving." Just as then, we still gather with friends, give thanks, and eat!

QUICK CHECK

Cause and Effect **Why did the Pilgrims hold a thanksgiving feast?**

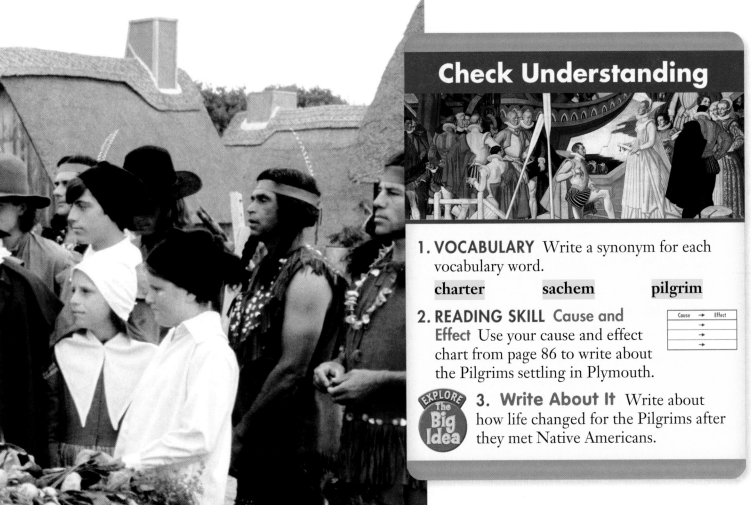

Check Understanding

1. **VOCABULARY** Write a synonym for each vocabulary word.

   charter   sachem   pilgrim

2. **READING SKILL** Cause and Effect Use your cause and effect chart from page 86 to write about the Pilgrims settling in Plymouth.

Cause	→	Effect
	→	
	→	
	→	

3. **Write About It** Write about how life changed for the Pilgrims after they met Native Americans.

EXPLORE The Big Idea

Vocabulary

Number a paper from 1 to 4. Beside each number write the word from the list below that matches the description.

navigation   empire

frontier   cash crop

1. Plants grown to be sold for profit

2. A large area in which different groups of people are controlled by one ruler or government

3. The far edge of a settled area

4. Finding direction and following routes at sea

Comprehension and Critical Thinking

5. Why were Europeans willing to pay a lot for products from Asia?

6. Why did the Pilgrims seek permission to leave England?

7. Why did Columbus return to Spain in 1493 with Taíno people?

8. Reading Skill How did de Soto's expedition hurt Native Americans?

9. Critical Thinking Why was the Northwest Passage important?

10. Critical Thinking How was the society of New Spain different from the society in Jamestown?

Skill

Understand Latitude and Longitude

Write a complete sentence to answer each question.

11. What are the coordinates on the map for Mexico City?

12. Santa Fe is about how many degrees north of Mexico City?

Southwest United States and Mexico: Latitude and Longitude

⊛ National capital
★ State capital

40°N

Santa Fe ★

OK ★ Oklahoma City

AZ   NM
★ Phoenix

TX
Austin ★

30°N

Gulf of Mexico

PACIFIC OCEAN

MEXICO

N
W ⊛ E
S

115°W   Gulf of California

20°N

0   250   500 miles
0   250   500 kilometers

Mexico City ⊛

105°W   95°W

Illinois Standards Achievement Test Preparation

> ### From a letter written by Don Miguel Costansó from the Port of San Diego
> ### June 28, 1769
>
> Having recently arrived . . . many are the things to be attended to at one time: the care of our own defenses occupied . . . everyone; the rations and attendance of the sick occupies others; also the firewood and water. . . . In the new quarters we also built [a] pole stockade for our security and put up some large sheds in order to cover the provisions and equipment. . . . In time of drought as now, the water of the wells which were dug by the men . . . is very salty and only in an urgent case of necessity is one able to drink it and then with danger to his health.

1

Where was Don Miguel Costansó when he wrote this letter?

Ⓐ San Francisco
Ⓑ San Diego
Ⓒ Portland
Ⓓ at sea

2

Which of the following is the best description of life at the Port of San Diego?

Ⓐ People hardly ever worked.
Ⓑ There was a large supply of food and water.
Ⓒ People worked very hard.
Ⓓ Everyone was constantly sick.

3

What is the purpose of the pole stockade?

Ⓐ Entertainment
Ⓑ Food
Ⓒ Security
Ⓓ Hide provisions

4

What seems to be the most dangerous condition in the Port of San Diego?

Ⓐ Little water
Ⓑ Bad weather
Ⓒ Too much food
Ⓓ No firewood

Activities

What happens when people from different cultures first meet?

Write About the Big Idea

FOLDABLES™
Study Organizer

Descriptive Journal Entry
Use the Unit 2 foldable to help you write a journal entry that answers the Big Idea question, "What happens when different cultures first meet?" Use the notes you wrote under each tab in the foldable. Decide whether to write your entry from "Before," "During" or "After" the cultures meet. Decide which cultures meet and when the meeting takes place. Describe the setting in your journal entry.

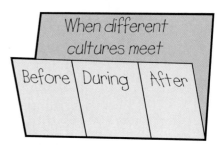

When different cultures meet

Before | During | After

Make a Photo Collage

Work individually to make a photo collage of the Columbian Exchange.

1. Study the examples on page 65 of food and animals that made up the Columbian Exchange.

2. Choose one example and use magazines, newspapers, or the Internet to find photos of that food or animal.

3. Make a photo collage of the ways that food or animals are used today.

When you finish your collage, present it to your class. Discuss what you have learned about the food or animal you chose.

Chocolate Today

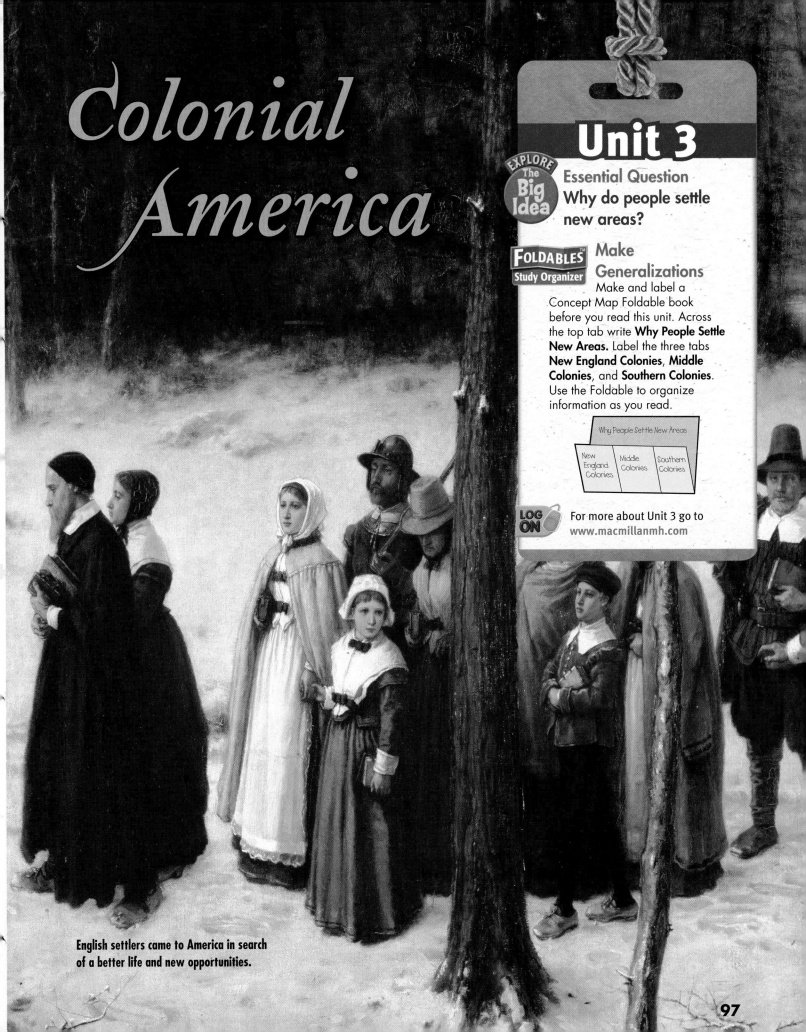

Colonial America

EXPLORE The Big Idea

Essential Question
Why do people settle new areas?

FOLDABLES Study Organizer

Make Generalizations
Make and label a Concept Map Foldable book before you read this unit. Across the top tab write **Why People Settle New Areas.** Label the three tabs **New England Colonies, Middle Colonies,** and **Southern Colonies.** Use the Foldable to organize information as you read.

Why People Settle New Areas

| New England Colonies | Middle Colonies | Southern Colonies |

LOG ON
For more about Unit 3 go to www.macmillanmh.com

English settlers came to America in search of a better life and new opportunities.

PEOPLE, PLACES, AND EVENTS

Anne Hutchinson

Metacomet

Portsmouth, Rhode Island

1638
Anne Hutchinson establishes a settlement in Rhode Island.

New England

1675
King Philip's War takes place in New England.

1625   1650   1675   1700

In 1638 **Anne Hutchinson** and her followers founded the religious settlement of **Portsmouth, Rhode Island**.

Today you can visit Founders Brook Park in Portsmouth, where Hutchinson first settled.

In 1675 **Metacomet**, also called King Philip, led Native Americans in a war against **New England** colonists.

Today you can visit the scene of a famous battle in South Deerfield, Massachusetts.

LOG ON

For more about People, Places, and Events, visit
www.macmillanmh.com

Benjamin Franklin

Andrew Bryan

Philadelphia, Pennsylvania

1749 Benjamin Franklin founds the University of Pennsylvania.

Savannah, Georgia

1788 Andrew Bryan founds the First African Baptist Church in Savannah, Georgia.

1725　　　　　1750　　　　　1775　　　　　1800

Benjamin Franklin founded the **University of Pennsylvania** in Philadelphia, Pennsylvania.

Today you can see statues honoring Franklin in Philadelphia.

In 1788 **Andrew Bryan**, an enslaved person, founded the **First African Baptist Church**.

Today you can see the African Baptist Church building in Savannah, Georgia.

NEW ENGLAND

Lesson 1

VOCABULARY

covenant p. 102

common p. 102

tolerate p. 103

fundamental p. 103

slavery p. 104

READING SKILL

Make Generalizations
Copy the chart below. As you read, fill it in to make a generalization about Puritans.

Text Clues	What You Know	Generalization

Illinois Learning Standards

15.D.2a, 16.A.2c, 16.B.2a(W), 16.C.2b(W), 16.E.2a(W), 17.A.2a, 17.A.2b, 17.B.2b

This saltbox house shows the style of homes in New England during the 1600s.

Visual Preview

How did differences shape New England?

A Puritans went to New England for religious freedom and governed themselves.

B Settlers who disagreed with Puritan life established new colonies.

C Wars between settlers and Native Americans broke out in New England.

MASSACHUSETTS BAY COMPANY

In June 1630, 300 hungry and exhausted passengers aboard the ship Arabella *arrived in Massachusetts Bay.* Arabella *led a fleet of 11 ships with about 1,000 passengers.*

Most of the people aboard the ships entering Massachusetts Bay were Puritans. Unlike the Pilgrims, Puritans didn't want to separate from the Church of England—they wanted to change the church. King James of England and many church leaders were furious and jailed some of the Puritans. When the Puritans were freed, many decided to leave England.

In 1629 a group of wealthy Puritans obtained a charter for the Massachusetts Bay Company. This company owned land in New England.

Puritans Arrive

To avoid the hardships of the Pilgrims, the Puritans brought more supplies, including horses and a herd of cows. They also arrived during warm weather instead of the beginning of winter.

The Puritans' charter allowed them to govern themselves. They held elections at town hall meetings, but only white men who owned property could vote. John Winthrop was elected the first governor.

Winthrop wrote about building "a city upon a hill" that would show how God wanted people to live. The Puritans named their first settlement Boston. By 1640 about 20,000 colonists lived near the shores of the Charles and Mystic rivers, which help form the peninsula of Boston.

QUICK CHECK

Make Generalizations **Why did Puritans come to New England?**

A New England town hall meeting ▶

LIFE IN NEW ENGLAND

Religion was so important to the Puritans that every member of the community had to enter a **covenant**, or contract, with the church. In this agreement the family promised to follow the rules of the Puritan church. Those who didn't follow the rules usually were forced to leave the colony.

Village Life

In the center of each Puritan village was a grassy area called the village **common**. The nearby meeting house also served as a church. At town meetings, issues were discussed and decisions were made by a majority vote.

Puritan adults treated young people like grown-ups. Children were expected to work hard to help their families and the community. Girls spun wool, made soap, cooked, and did household jobs. Boys cut wood, cared for animals, and worked on farms.

The Puritans wanted children to read the Bible, so every village had a school. The town chose one person, usually a religious leader, to teach the children. Schooling was so important to Puritans that they established Harvard College in 1636, six years after they arrived.

A New England Village

Mill

Inn

Meeting House

Blacksmith

Stocks

Barrel maker

Common

Rebels Start New Colonies

Even though each person entered a covenant, some people still disagreed with Puritan leaders. These disagreements led to the establishment of other colonies.

One person who disagreed with Puritan leaders was Roger Williams. He believed that government should **tolerate** people with different religious views. To tolerate means to allow people to have beliefs or behaviors that are different from others. Puritans accused Williams of spreading "new and dangerous opinions" and tried to silence him. After he was forced to leave the colony, Williams moved south where he lived with the Narragansett. In 1636 he bought land from the Narragansett and founded the settlement of Providence in what later became Rhode Island. It was the first colony to allow freedom of religion.

Anne Hutchinson was another person who disagreed with Puritan leaders. She told Puritans who met in her home that people should understand the Bible in their own way. They should not let ministers tell them what to think. She said:

> He who has God's grace in his heart cannot go astray.
>
> —ANNE HUTCHINSON

Puritan leaders put her on trial and forced Hutchinson out of the Massachusetts Bay Colony in 1638. She and her followers founded the settlement of Portsmouth in Rhode Island.

Diagram Skill

What kind of work did villagers in early New England do?

Primary Sources

It is Ordered . . . that there shall be yearly two General Assemblies . . . the first shall be called the Court of Election, wherein shall be yearly chosen from time to time . . . one to be chosen as Governor . . . shall have the power to administer justice according to the Laws here established . . . .

A section from The Fundamental Orders of Connecticut

by Thomas Hooker, 1639

Write About It It is 1639 and you have founded a new colony. Write a set of rules your settlers can use to govern themselves.

Thomas Hooker also disagreed with Puritan beliefs. He thought that churches should be independent from one another and should choose their own leaders. In 1636 he led a group of settlers to the fertile Connecticut River valley. The rich soil was perfect for farming. There, he helped the settlers draw up a set of **fundamental**, or basic, rules to govern themselves. Read a section of *The Fundamental Orders of Connecticut* above.

QUICK CHECK

Make Generalizations What generalization can you make about Williams, Hooker, and Hutchinson?

C NATIVE AMERICAN CONFLICTS

The Wampanoag and Pequot were two of the Native American groups living in the New England area. At first the Wampanoag helped English colonists, and the two groups were peaceful neighbors. However, later colonists ignored the rights of Native Americans. As colonists settled across New England, groups such as the powerful Pequot did not want colonists to take their land.

The Pequot War

In 1637 war finally broke out. In a surprise attack, settlers surrounded a Pequot village in Mystic, Connecticut, and set fire to it. Hundreds of Pequot men, women, and children were killed as they ran from their homes. Many more were captured. Those who were captured were sold into **slavery**. Slavery is the practice of treating people as property and forcing them to work.

By 1638 the once powerful Pequot had lost hundreds of their people. The defeated Pequot gave away the rights to their land and went to live with other nearby Native American groups. After that, English settlers moved into areas of present-day New Hampshire, Vermont, and Maine.

King Philip's War

Massasoit, the Wampanoag leader who helped the Pilgrims, died in 1661. For 40 years he had kept peace with the colonists. This would soon change. English colonists continued to arrive during the 1600s. The new colonists seized land that had belonged to the Wampanoag for centuries.

▼ Settlers destroy a Pequot fort in Connecticut.

THE NEW ENGLAND COLONIES

0   50   100 miles
0   50   100 kilometers

NEW FRANCE

MAINE (part of Massachusetts)

Lake Champlain   ABENAKI   PENOBSCOT

Kennebec River

VERMONT (claimed by New Hampshire and New York)

Connecticut River

NEW HAMPSHIRE (1680)

Hudson River

MASSACHUSETTS (1630)   Boston   Massachusetts Bay   Plymouth   ATLANTIC OCEAN

PEQUOT   Cape Cod   Cape Cod Bay

Hartford   Providence

CONNECTICUT (1636)   WAMPANOAG   Portsmouth

RHODE ISLAND (1636)

Long Island   NARRAGANSETT

Long Island Sound

| PEQUOT | Native American group |

Map Skill

LOCATION What direction was Boston from Metacomet's land?

The new leader of the Wampanoag was Massasoit's son, Metacomet. Called "Philip" by the English colonial governor, Metacomet became known as "King Philip" to the colonists.

Metacomet wanted to stop the English from taking more land. He sent messengers to his enemies, the Narragansett, asking for their help against the settlers. They refused, but other Native American groups across New England joined Metacomet.

King Philip's War began in 1675 and lasted for more than a year. It was one of the bloodiest wars ever fought in North America. Metacomet's fighters attacked 52 towns and killed more than 600 colonists. Entire towns were burned. Crops were destroyed.

The colonists fought in the style of the Native Americans. They hid in the forests and launched surprise attacks. They burned the villages of the Native Americans.

Finally, in August 1676, Native American scouts helped colonists trap Metacomet in a swamp in Rhode Island. The Wampanoag leader was killed by a Native American helping the English colonists.

With King Philip's death, the war ended. About 4,000 Native Americans had been killed and many more, including Metacomet's wife and son, had been sold into slavery. Native American power in New England never recovered.

Native Americans used war clubs in battles against the settlers. ▼

The English used a sword like this one during battles. ▲

QUICK CHECK

Make Generalizations **Why did colonists fight in a style like Native Americans?**

Check Understanding

1. **VOCABULARY** Write a paragraph about Puritans using the word that means "agreement."

   covenant   tolerate

   common   fundamental

2. **READING SKILL** Make Generalizations Use your chart from page 100 to help you write about Puritans.

Text Clues	What You Know	Generalization

3. **Write About It** Write about why Native Americans wanted to stop colonists from settling new areas.

VOCABULARY

patroon p. 107

proprietor p. 108

READING SKILL

Make Generalizations

Copy the chart below. As you read, fill it in to make a generalization about why the Middle Colonies had a diverse population.

Text Clues	What You Know	Generalization

Illinois Learning Standards

14.B.2, 15.D.2a, 16.B.2a(W), 16.C.2b(W), 16.D.2(W), 17.A.2a, 17.C.2b, 18.A.2,

The Middle Colonies

New Amsterdam traders and merchants

Visual Preview

What factors influenced the development of the Middle Colonies?

A New Netherland was a center for trade filled with people from all over the world.

B Settlers from many different cultures came to New York and New Jersey.

C William Penn showed the world that a diverse population could live in peace.

A NEW NETHERLAND

In 1609 Henry Hudson claimed the land that is now New York for the Dutch. Then in 1621 the Dutch West India Company decided to set up a colony there. They called it New Netherland.

New Amsterdam, present-day Manhattan, was one of the most important settlements in New Netherland. The Dutch had bought the land from the Manahates. New Amsterdam had a great natural harbor, which made it perfect for trade. The colony's many natural resources included timber, fish, and fur-bearing animals. It soon was filled with sailors and traders from all over the world. The Dutch were tolerant of different religions and ethnic groups.

To attract new settlers, the Dutch West India Company offered land grants to **patroons** in 1629. Patroons were wealthy Dutch men who agreed to bring 50 people to the colony. However, because settlers had to clear the land themselves and share their crops with the patroons, the system did not attract many colonists.

The English Take New Netherland

In 1664 King Charles II of England gave his brother James, the Duke of York, a gift. This gift included all the land between the Connecticut and the Delaware Rivers, including New Netherland. The Duke of York arrived in the harbor of New Amsterdam with four warships. Peter Stuyvesant, the fiery governor of New Netherland, wanted to fight them. The Dutch colonists had no interest in fighting the English. New Netherland fell without firing a shot. The English renamed the colony New York, and New Amsterdam became New York City. The Duke of York gave part of New York to two friends who named it New Jersey in honor of the English island of Jersey. New York and New Jersey would become important English colonies.

QUICK CHECK

Make Generalizations What generalization can be made about the patroon system?

EVENT

Around 1637 Swedish colonists founded New Sweden along Delaware Bay. **Peter Stuyvesant** believed the land they settled belonged to the Dutch. In 1655 Stuyvesant captured New Sweden. Today it is part of New Jersey, Pennsylvania, and Delaware.

Peter Stuyvesant

Through trade, New York and New Jersey soon developed strong economies. Like New York's Hudson River, New Jersey's Delaware River became a major river for trade. The colony also had flat farmland and a mild climate. With rich soil and mild weather, agriculture kept New Jersey's economy strong.

Groups from Many Lands

Instead of being owned by the king or a company, both New York and New Jersey were owned by a man or a small group of men. They were called **proprietors**. These owners appointed the governors and ran the colonies as businesses.

To attract new settlers, proprietors offered newcomers free land. They also promised religious freedom and gave settlers a voice in their government. What was the downside? Settlers had to pay a tax. Still, a diverse population of German, Dutch, Irish, English Quaker, and Swedish settlers came to the colonies from Europe.

▼ Because farms grew so much corn, wheat, and oats, the Middle Colonies were known as the "Breadbasket of the Colonies."

Daily Life

Have you ever heard the phrase "sharing is caring?" Well, sharing is not only caring, it is also very smart. The settlers of New York and New Jersey learned new skills by sharing their knowledge. Swedes, for example, taught people how to build cabins out of logs. Scots shared farming ideas with Germans. Native Americans taught the colonists how to hunt for whales off the shores of Long Island.

The new settlers had to work hard to earn a living. Some grew corn, wheat, barley, or oats. Others worked as merchants, loggers, shipbuilders, or ironworkers.

Walking in colonial New York City, people heard different languages and tasted foods from many different countries in restaurants and homes. People also practiced many different religions. In both New York and New Jersey, Catholics, and Protestants worshipped freely. For these groups, life was better in the Middle Colonies than it had been in Europe or New England.

However, life was not better for everyone in the Middle Colonies. When the English took over New Netherland, free Africans had been working in the colony since 1626. But that came to an end in 1690. The English wrote new laws that said that even free Africans could be enslaved.

QUICK CHECK

Make Generalizations **What generalization is made about religion in New York and New Jersey?**

▼ A New York City street in the 1700s

Benjamin West painted *William Penn's Treaty with the Indians.*

C PENNSYLVANIA AND DELAWARE

William Penn came from a rich family that belonged to the Church of England. He left England to establish an American colony and became a member of a religious group called the Society of Friends, or Quakers.

Penn's Colony

Fortunately for Penn, King Charles II owed money to his father. After the death of Penn's father, the king paid his debt by giving William Penn a large piece of land in the Middle Colonies. Penn named the colony Pennsylvania, or "Penn's Woods," in honor of his father. He called his first settlement Philadelphia. In Greek the word means "city of brotherly love." Philadelphia soon became a center for trade along the Delaware River.

Like the Puritans, the Quakers in England had been jailed for their beliefs. Penn wanted a place where they could worship without fear.

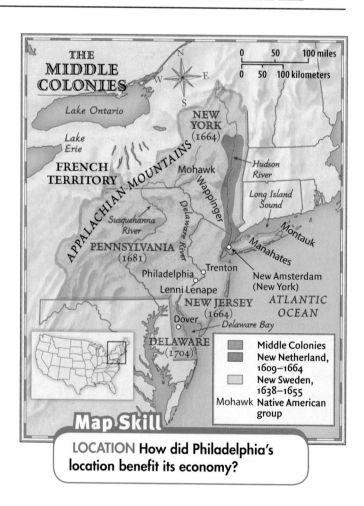

THE MIDDLE COLONIES

0   50   100 miles
0   50   100 kilometers

Lake Ontario

NEW YORK (1664)

Lake Erie

FRENCH TERRITORY

APPALACHIAN MOUNTAINS

Mohawk

Hudson River

Long Island Sound

Susquehanna River

Delaware River

Wappinger

Montauk

PENNSYLVANIA (1681)

Manahates

Philadelphia   Trenton

New Amsterdam (New York)

Lenni Lenape

NEW JERSEY (1664)

ATLANTIC OCEAN

Dover   Delaware Bay

DELAWARE (1704)

Middle Colonies
New Netherland, 1609–1664
New Sweden, 1638–1655
Mohawk Native American group

Map Skill

LOCATION **How did Philadelphia's location benefit its economy?**

When Penn wrote his *Frame of Government of Pennsylvania* in 1682, he included in it the right to free worship and the right to a trial by jury.

Settlers from Different Lands

Pennsylvania attracted people from a variety of religions and backgrounds. Many Germans, for example, came to Pennsylvania to escape wars in their homeland. Other German immigrants belonged to a religious group called the Mennonites. They were called "plain people" because they lived and dressed simply. German settlers in Pennsylvania are often called "Pennsylvania Dutch." The reason for this could be that the word for "German" in the German language is *Deutsch*. One German settler wrote about his voyage in 1683:

> **"**My company consisted of many sorts of people. . . . They were not only different in respect to their occupations, but were also of such different religions and behaviors that I might . . . compare the ship . . . with Noah's Ark.**"**

In addition to settlers from Germany and England, Pennsylvania attracted many Scots-Irish people. The Scots-Irish were people from Scotland who settled in Ireland in the early 1600s. They left Ireland in search of jobs and land to farm—in short, a better life.

Delaware

The southeastern part of Pennsylvania was called the Three Lower Counties. Before the English settled there, the region had been a part of New Sweden. The colonists of the Three Lower Counties wanted to make their own laws. In 1704 Penn allowed this area to elect its own assembly under the control of Pennsylvania's governor. Today this area is the state of Delaware.

QUICK CHECK

Make Generalizations **What generalization is made about the Mennonites?**

Check Understanding

1. **VOCABULARY** Write a sentence that explains the difference between the two words below.

   patroon   **proprietor**

2. **READING SKILL** Make Generalizations Use your chart from page 106 to write about why the Middle Colonies had a diverse population.

Text Clues	What You Know	Generalization

3. **Write About It** Write about why many Scots-Irish people settled in the Middle Colonies.

The Southern Colonies

Lesson 3

VOCABULARY

plantation p. 114

indigo p. 114

debtor p. 115

READING SKILL

Make Generalizations
Copy the chart below. As you read, fill it in to make a generalization about the economy of the Southern Colonies.

Text Clues	What You Know	Generalization

Illinois Learning Standards

5.D.2a, 16.A.2b, 16.A.2c, 16.B.2a(W), 16.C.2b(W), 16.D.2(W), 17.A.2a, 17.C.2b,

Currier & Ives painted this Virginia plantation.

Visual Preview

How did the Southern Colonies differ from other settlements?

A Catholics and Protestants found religious freedom in Maryland.

B Carolina split into north and south, while Georgia started as a debtor colony.

C In Georgia, colonists made friends with the Creek and grew rice.

Ⓐ MARYLAND

If you started a colony, how would you attract settlers? Virginia advertised the benefits of settling there. These stories drew many settlers and encouraged the English to establish more colonies in the South.

George Calvert was a wealthy lord who was well-liked. But he became a Catholic in England at a time when that was illegal. Luckily, King Charles I liked Calvert, also known as Lord Baltimore, and granted him the land north of Virginia along the Chesapeake Bay. Calvert dreamed of starting a colony for Catholics, but he died before he could carry out his dream.

A Colony for Catholics

Calvert's son, Cecilius, actually founded the colony, but he stayed in England to make sure the king supported the colony. Cecilius believed Catholics and Protestants could live together in peace. Leonard Calvert, his brother, became the first governor of Maryland. Cecilius and Leonard ran Maryland like a business. Under their rule, the colony grew wealthy, with large tobacco farms dotting the shores of the bay. The city of Baltimore became a busy port.

▲ George Calvert

Religion and Democracy

Conflicts between Catholics and Protestants soon arose. Lord Baltimore feared Maryland would become a Protestant colony. He proposed that Protestants and Catholics should have the right to worship freely. In 1649 the assembly passed the Toleration Act, allowing religious freedom for Christians. It declared that Catholics and Protestants could not threaten one another.

QUICK CHECK

Make Generalizations **What generalization can you make about the Calverts?**

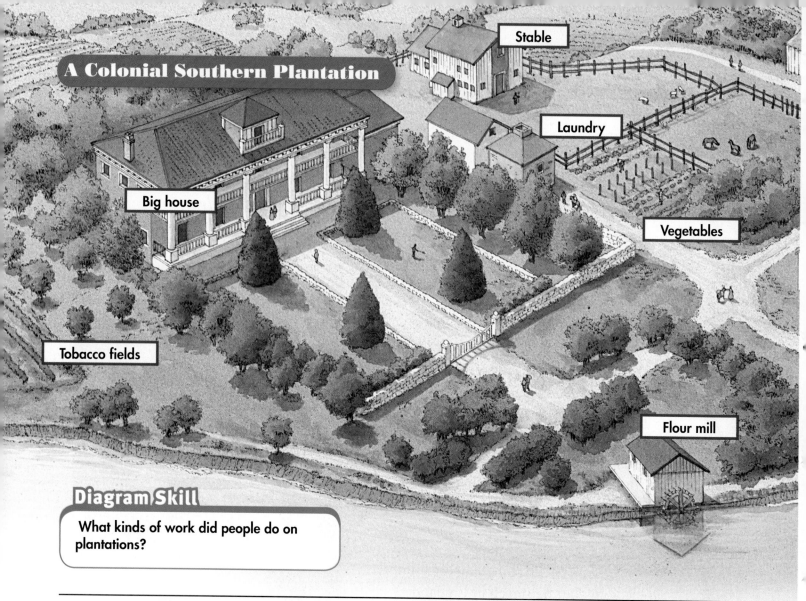

A Colonial Southern Plantation

Stable

Laundry

Big house

Vegetables

Tobacco fields

Flour mill

Diagram Skill

What kinds of work did people do on plantations?

B CAROLINA AND GEORGIA

King Charles II gave eight proprietors a charter to found Carolina in 1663. Seven years later, the first big city in the Southern Colonies, Charles Town, was founded in Carolina. Charles Town's natural harbor, warm climate, and natural resources made it a center for agriculture and trade. Wealthy colonists built **plantations** outside the city. Plantations are large farms that grow one main crop as a cash crop. Plantations in Carolina grew tobacco and rice. They also grew **indigo**, a plant used to make blue dye. Plantations were like small villages. Look at the diagram of a plantation above.

North and South Separate

Colonists who settled the land of northern Carolina grew tobacco and sold forest products such as timber and tar. The economy in northern Carolina grew slowly due to the lack of a good harbor. In southern Carolina the harbor in Charles Town allowed for easy trade. It was discovered that rice grew well in the coastal lowlands of the southern part of the colony. Rice soon became the leading cash crop. In 1729 these differences in colonial life in Carolina resulted in the colony splitting into North Carolina and South Carolina.

Slave quarters

Carpenter

Blacksmith

> The Colony of Georgia . . . shall [supply] . . . England . . . with raw Silk, Wine, Oil, Dyes, Drugs, and many other materials for manufactures. . . .

Oglethorpe was a decorated general and became a member of the English Parliament in 1722. Because of his military experience, Oglethorpe received a charter to start a colony south of the Carolinas. King George II wanted a military man to run the colony because England, France, and Spain had all claimed this land south of the Carolinas. Oglethorpe would protect the Southern Colonies from the Spanish to the south and the French who had settlements to the west.

In 1732, 116 men, women, and children left London and set sail for the newest English colony in America. It was named Georgia, after King George II.

Settling Georgia

British General James Oglethorpe had a great idea. What if **debtors** could be sent to the colonies? Debtors are people who owe money but cannot repay it. At that time debtors were put in prison. Oglethorpe thought that instead of wasting away in prison, debtors could be free to live and work in Georgia. He thought slavery would not be necessary with all the debtors to do the work. Oglethorpe also thought that Georgia had the right conditions for making products such as silk that were in high demand in England. He said:

QUICK CHECK

Make Generalizations Make a generalization about why Carolina split into two colonies.

115

Oglethorpe understood that for his new colony to succeed, he needed to have peace with the Native Americans in the area. A Creek group, the Yamacraw, lived near Yamacraw Bluff, where Oglethorpe planned to build his first settlement, Savannah. Oglethorpe obtained Yamacraw Bluff from Chief Tomochichi, the leader of the Yamacraw. Tomochichi also helped the colonists establish peaceful relations with other Creek groups.

Tomochichi remained a lifelong friend of the English colonists. In 1734 Oglethorpe invited Tomochichi to go to England and meet King George II. Tomochichi gave the king some eagle feathers as a token of peace. Before Tomochichi died in 1739, he told his people to remember the kindness of the king of England and said he hoped they would always be friendly to the colonists.

Mary Musgrove also helped the Creek and the colonists become friends. Her mother came from a powerful Creek family. Her father was English. Musgrove had learned the Creek language and customs from her mother. When Oglethorpe arrived in Savannah, she became the translator for the settlers and the Creek.

Map Skill

LOCATION Which Native American groups lived in South Carolina?

James Oglethorpe's first meeting with Chief Tomochichi at the first Georgia settlement, Savannah ▶

▲ James Oglethorpe

Early Failures

Georgia got off to a difficult start. Oglethorpe had planned to raise silkworms, but the silk industry failed. Oglethorpe's plan for England's debtors also failed, because few debtors came.

Georgia Expands

While few debtors settled in Georgia, many other people did. The colony promised freedom of religion to all Protestant Christians. Colonists were also given free land to use for 10 years. This attracted settlers who were seeking a better life.

Hundreds of poor people came from Great Britain. Religious refugees from Germany and Switzerland also settled in Georgia. The colony soon had the highest percentage of non-British settlers compared to any other British colony in the Americas.

The Colony Changes

In the beginning, the colonists of Georgia grew tobacco. Later rice became the most profitable cash crop. Until 1750 Georgia was the only English colony that did not allow slavery. Oglethorpe had planned for the settlers to do all the work. However, there were not enough workers so some colonists smuggled enslaved workers into Georgia from South Carolina.

Enslaved Africans worked on the rice plantations of South Carolina. After slavery became legal in Georgia in 1750, many planters from South Carolina moved into Georgia, bringing enslaved workers with them. In the 1760s Georgians brought captives directly from Africa. By 1775 Georgia had 18,000 enslaved Africans.

QUICK CHECK

Make Generalizations **What generalization can you make about the growth of slavery in Georgia?**

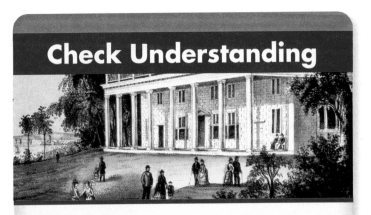

Check Understanding

1. **VOCABULARY** Write a paragraph about the Southern Colonies using two of the words below.

   plantation   indigo   debtor

2. **READING SKILL** Make Generalizations
   Use your chart from page 112 to write about the economy of the Southern Colonies.

Text Clues	What You Know	Generalization

3. **Write About It** Write about the reasons settlers came to the Southern Colonies.

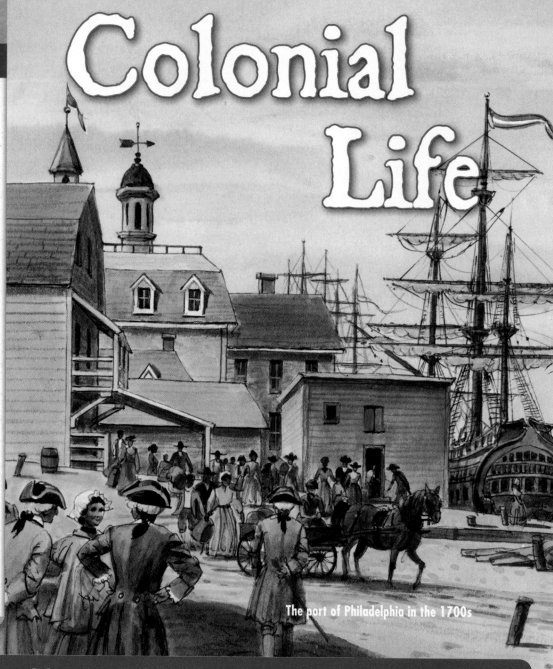

Lesson 4

VOCABULARY

slave trade p. 119

apprentice p. 120

growth rate p. 121

Great Awakening p. 121

backcountry p. 122

READING SKILL

Make Generalizations
Use the chart to make a generalization about the quality of life in colonial towns compared to life on the frontier.

Text Clues	What You Know	Generalization

Illinois Learning Standards

15.D.2b, 16.A.2a, 16.B.2a(W), 16.C.2a(W), 16.C.2b(W), 16.E.2a(W), 17.A.2b, 18.A.2, 18.C.2

Colonial Life

The port of Philadelphia in the 1700s

Visual Preview

How did economic needs affect life in the colonies?

A Many came to the colonies for a better life, while others came against their will.

B Colonists learned crafts, while the colonies grew rapidly and changed.

C As colonists settled the West, they came into conflict with Native American groups.

Ⓐ WHY THEY CAME

Living conditions in Europe during the 1700s were miserable for many people. Some fled wars or food shortages in their homelands to settle in the English colonies. They were drawn by the promise of cheap land, economic opportunity, and religious freedom.

The dangerous journey across the Atlantic Ocean took between two and three months. It was a terrible time for those aboard a ship. The ships were crowded, damp, and filthy. Storms sank many vessels. Ships often ran out of food and water. Diseases spread quickly and killed many of the people on ships sailing to the colonies from Europe.

Enslaved Africans were crowded into the holds of slave ships.

Captives and Servants

Conditions for African captives were even more dreadful. Every part of the **slave trade**, or the business of buying and selling people, was designed to bring profits to the traders. On ships, captives were chained together and crammed into spaces where they could barely sit up. One out of seven captives died from disease, starvation, or poor treatment during the journey.

Indentured servants were people who chose to come to the colonies but could not pay their way. They contracted, or agreed, to work for a colonist usually for five to seven years to repay the price of the voyage. Indentured servants also received food, clothing, and shelter in return for their work. However, their living conditions were often harsh and their work, especially in the fields, was difficult. When their contracts ended, indentured servants often received farmland, animals, and supplies of lumber and tools.

QUICK CHECK

Make Generalizations **What generalization can you make about the voyage across the Atlantic Ocean?**

B DAILY LIFE

Most colonial families worked on farms. Men planted crops and hunted. Women did household work such as cooking, gardening, sewing, cleaning, spinning, and weaving. Children did chores such as feeding chickens, milking cows, gathering eggs, and cleaning. When they were not helping at home or studying, children played with marbles, kites, and jump ropes.

Learning a Trade

To learn a skill, a young person could become an **apprentice**. An apprentice is someone who works for a skilled person and in exchange, learns a trade or craft. After studying and practicing, an apprentice might become a silversmith, printer, or barrel maker, for example. Apprentices were not paid, but they received meals and housing while they learned their trade. At first only boys were allowed to be apprentices. After 1647 girls became apprentices in such trades as printing.

Early Communities

Colonists often combined work with play. An entire community, for example, would gather to build a house for a newly married couple. Examples of other community activities were cornhusking competitions and

A cabinetmaker teaches his young apprentice how to make a cabinet.

▲ A chest of drawers from the 1700s

quilting bees. At quilting bees neighbors sewed together pieces of cloth to make a bedspread.

The Colonies Grow and Change

Trade along the Atlantic coast led to population growth in the colonies. The population **growth rate** from 1700 to 1750 was about 450 percent. The growth rate is a year-to-year change expressed as a percentage. Philadelphia was the largest city in the colonies. By 1750 it had grown to almost 20,000 people. Benjamin Franklin did much to help the city grow. He established the first fire department and public library. Franklin also improved the city's police department and postal system.

Religion Changes

Religion also changed in the colonies during the 1700s. Growing interest in religion led to a period known as the **Great Awakening**. Preachers such as Jonathan Edwards and George Whitefield spread their message with a dramatic and emotional style. The more dramatic the sermon, the more people attended. During the Great Awakening, less formal church services taught that all people should have religious experiences.

During this time, many people changed from Puritanism to other forms of worship. For example, some Puritans became Baptists or Methodists. Some New England Baptist groups welcomed enslaved Africans at their church meetings.

QUICK CHECK

Make Generalization **What generalization can you make about working in the colonies?**

Citizenship

Working for the Common Good

What are some ways citizens can work for the common good, or for something that benefits everyone? Benjamin Franklin believed good deeds were best accomplished by working together. In 1727 Franklin and his friends formed a club that created many organizations to benefit Philadelphia, including the first volunteer fire department. You can work for the common good by becoming involved in solving a community problem or volunteering for an organization that helps others.

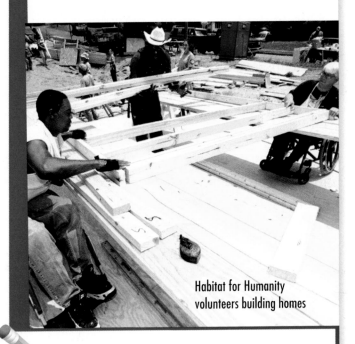

Habitat for Humanity volunteers building homes

Write About It Write a list of five projects you and your classmates can do to make your school a better place for everyone.

A Cherokee chief

In 1715 the Yamasee, with their allies the Muscogee and Choctaw, attacked the colonists, causing many settlers to flee to other colonies. The Cherokee, however, agreed to help the colonists in exchange for weapons and other goods. The Yamasee lost the war and fled to Florida. The Cherokee then became the most powerful Native American group in the Carolinas.

QUICK CHECK

Make Generalizations **Why did fighting break out between the colonists and Native Americans in the backcountry?**

During the 1740s, groups of settlers began to move into the area between the Appalachian Mountains and the Atlantic Coastal Plain. This area was known as the **backcountry**. Land in the backcountry cost much less money than land on the Atlantic Coastal Plain. Most of these settlers came from Ireland, Scotland, and Germany. Families in the backcountry built log cabins and cleared areas in the forests to grow corn and wheat. Life was hard, but people still managed to have fun. Like other colonists, they held dances, quilting contests, and other competitions.

The Yamasee War

Many Native Americans also lived in the backcountry. The Yamasee were originally friends of the Carolina colonists. The Yamasee complained when colonists began taking too much land and breaking their promises.

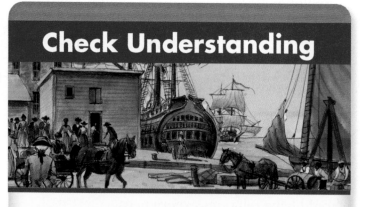

Check Understanding

1. **VOCABULARY** Write a paragraph about the colonial way of life using the words below.

   apprentice   backcountry

2. **READING SKILL** Make Generalizations Use your chart from page 118 to write about why people changed to new forms of worship during the Great Awakening.

Text Clues	What You Know	Generalization

3. **Write About It** Write about why German, Scottish, and Irish immigrants who came to the colonies in the 1700s settled in the backcountry.

Map and Globe Skills

Use a Historical Map

VOCABULARY

historical map

As you have read, colonists in New England lived along rivers and the Atlantic coast. They used these waterways for transportation. Over time, this land became too expensive for many colonists, so many people began moving inland where land was less expensive. You can see this movement of people by looking at a **historical map**. This kind of map shows where events from the past took place.

Learn It

● Look at the map title and dates to find the map topic. Most historical maps have dates.

● Look at the map key to find out the meaning of symbols or shading on the map.

Try It

● Which parts of New England were settled between 1700 and 1760?

● Which color represents land settled between 1660 and 1700?

Apply It

● As you read the rest of this unit, look for other historical maps.

● Compare the information that is given in those maps with the information that you read in each lesson.

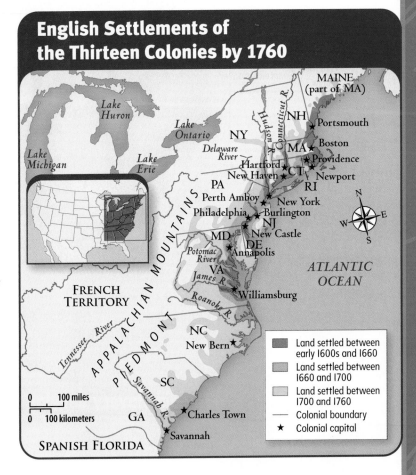

English Settlements of the Thirteen Colonies by 1760

MAINE (part of MA)

Lake Huron
Lake Ontario
Lake Michigan
Lake Erie

NH
Portsmouth
NY
MA
Boston
Providence
Delaware River
Hartford
New Haven
CT
Newport
RI
PA
Perth Amboy
New York
Philadelphia
Burlington
NJ
New Castle
MD
DE
Annapolis
Potomac River
VA
James R.
ATLANTIC OCEAN
Williamsburg
FRENCH TERRITORY
Roanoke R.
APPALACHIAN MOUNTAINS
Tennessee River
NC
New Bern
PIEDMONT
SC
Savannah R.
GA
Charles Town
Savannah
SPANISH FLORIDA

0   100 miles
0   100 kilometers

■ Land settled between early 1600s and 1660
■ Land settled between 1660 and 1700
■ Land settled between 1700 and 1760
— Colonial boundary
★ Colonial capital

SLAVERY IN THE COLONIES

VOCABULARY

slave codes p. 125

spiritual p. 127

READING SKILL

Make Generalizations

Copy the chart below. As you read, fill it in to make a generalization about why slavery was established in the thirteen colonies.

Text Clues	What You Know	Generalization

Illinois Learning Standards

15.D.2a, 16.A.2b, 16.A.2c, 16.B.2a(W), 16.C.2b(W), 17.A.2a, 17.C.2b, 17.D.2a

The first African captives arriving in Jamestown in 1619

Visual Preview

Why did slavery develop in the English Colonies?

A The supply of enslaved workers kept growing because of new laws.

B Slavery was more common on large plantations in the South than in the North.

C Enslaved Africans led rebellions on ships and in the colonies.

Slavery began when people started farming 10,000 years ago.
At that time most enslaved people were those who had lost a war.
Many had some legal rights. Slavery in the 1700s was different.

For a long time the English believed people who were not Christians could rightly be enslaved. If the captives converted to Christianity, then they would be set free. It didn't matter what color skin they had. But the Atlantic slave trade—the transporting of enslaved people from Africa to the Americas—changed that. Some Europeans became rich by kidnapping, transporting, and selling captive Africans. By the middle of the 1700s, more than 250,000 enslaved Africans had been brought to North America. Far more were brought to Brazil and the Caribbean Islands.

Slavery Becomes Legal

In 1641 Massachusetts became the first colony to make slavery legal. By 1751 Africans could legally be enslaved in all thirteen colonies.

Colonists believed that the use of enslaved workers was needed for the colonial economy to grow and stay strong. As a result, the demand for enslaved workers grew dramatically.

Laws called **slave codes** set rules of slavery. Some of the earliest Africans in the colonies were indentured servants. The slave codes ended that. These laws said that African captives brought to the colonies would have almost no rights.

The first slave laws said that people who were not Christians could be enslaved. Soon some Native Americans and Africans became Christians. But the demand for enslaved workers kept growing, so the colonists changed the laws. After that, any captive African could be enslaved, including Christians and children born to enslaved workers.

QUICK CHECK

Make Generalizations **Why did slave codes allow Christians to become enslaved?**

A slave auction

125

Enslaved Africans did many kinds of work, often depending on the economy of the colony where they lived. Some were skilled workers, such as carpenters, blacksmiths, cooks, and weavers. Other captive Africans worked as field hands or in the homes of slaveholders.

The Northern Colonies

In the North many enslaved Africans worked in New England's shipyards. In Rhode Island, Connecticut, and New York, enslaved workers did farm labor. Northern farms were generally small. Colonists in the North rarely owned more than one or two enslaved workers. However, many Northern colonists owned the slave ships. Before the 1770s most captive Africans were shipped to Rhode Island to be sold throughout the colonies.

New York had the largest enslaved population of the Northern colonies. In New York City, some people used enslaved workers in construction. Enslaved Africans even built the wall that gave Wall Street its name.

The Southern Colonies

Many Southern farms, on the other hand, were large and grew cash crops, especially tobacco. Both rice and tobacco required many workers to plant, tend, and harvest the crop. About one-fourth of white Southern farmers were slaveholders. Farms with a small number of captive Africans were more common than large plantations. Hundreds of enslaved people worked the fields on large plantations. In South Carolina by 1720, more than half of the colony's population was enslaved Africans.

▼ Reenactment of enslaved field work

A plantation celebration

African Culture

Despite brutal hardships, enslaved Africans carried on the culture from their homes in Africa. African words such as *banjo* and *gumbo*, for example, first came into the English language in the South.

Slave codes made it illegal for enslaved Africans to read or write. As a result, they often told traditional stories to their children and to each other. Many stories told how a clever animal, such as a fox, outsmarted a powerful person. Africans also created work songs, which they sang as they worked. **Spirituals**, the religious songs of enslaved Africans, have had a great influence on American music today. A number of spirituals are about freedom.

▲ This apprentice is learning how to make a basket.

QUICK CHECK

Make Generalizations **Why was the population of enslaved people higher in the Southern Colonies than in the Northern Colonies?**

Enslaved Africans had been kidnapped, forced to work for others, separated from their families, and often punished harshly. As a result, they looked for ways to fight back against the colonists. Some resisted slavery by slowing their work or by breaking or losing tools. Others escaped, hoping to find freedom in less settled areas. Some found freedom living among Native Americans and other runaway Africans in the backcountry. Some enslaved Africans who escaped hoped to find family members who had been sold away.

Slave Revolts

Enslaved Africans sometimes rebelled violently. Although rebellion was rare, it remained a constant fear among colonists. Twice within 30 years, slave rebellions alarmed the thirteen English colonies.

One of the first slave revolts was in New York City in 1712. During the revolt, about 25 Africans and 2 Native Americans launched a surprise attack. Armed with guns, hatchets, and swords, they set fire to a building and waited for a crowd to gather. Then they opened fire on the crowd killing several colonists. The colonists reacted quickly to this revolt and captured and killed most of the rebels.

The Stono Rebellion

Another revolt broke out in South Carolina in 1739. An enslaved African named Jemmy and about 20 of his followers stole guns and gunpowder from a warehouse in Stono, South Carolina, about 15 miles from Charles Town. They killed several colonists in Stono and marched down the road with a banner that read "Liberty!" As many as 100 enslaved workers joined them.

Captives who revolted at sea were often killed by the ship's crew. ▼

The group hoped to reach St. Augustine, a Spanish colony, where they had been promised freedom. However, a mob of plantation owners from South Carolina attacked them, killing about 40 of the rebels.

This reproduction shows the living conditions of enslaved workers.

QUICK CHECK

Summarize In what ways did enslaved Africans resist slavery?

Check Understanding

1. **VOCABULARY** Write two sentences about slavery in the English colonies using these vocabulary terms.

   slave code   **spiritual**

2. **READING SKILL Make Generalizations** Use your chart from page 124 to write about slavery in the colonies.

Text Clues	What You Know	Generalization

3. **Write About It** Why were Africans brought to the Americas in the 1700s?

VOCABULARY

triangular trade p. 132

Middle Passage p. 133

industry p. 134

READING SKILL

Make Generalizations

Copy the chart below. As you read, use it to make a generalization about English trade laws.

Text Clues	What You Know	Generalization

Illinois Learning Standards

15.D.2a, 16.A.2c, 16.B.2a(W), 16.C.2b(W), 17.A.2b, 17.C.2a, 17.C.2b, 18.A.2

Colonial Economies

A reenactment of coopers making colonial style barrels

Visual Preview

What influenced the development of colonial economies?

A Colonists ignored laws that England passed to regulate Colonial trade.

B Ships on the triangular trade routes moved cargo and enslaved Africans.

C Each colony developed an economy based on the resources of its region.

A COLONIAL TRADE

Between 1651 and 1764, England passed trade laws to control what and how the colonists could trade. The laws also controlled what colonists could make. To earn a profit, many colonists ignored the laws and turned to smuggling.

England wanted the colonists to buy their manufactured goods. For this reason, England made it illegal for the colonies to manufacture goods that competed with English goods. For example, it was illegal for the colonists to make hats, nails, and horseshoes. English trade laws, called the Navigation Acts, listed goods that the colonies could sell only to England or its colonies. These included farm products such as sugar, tobacco, lumber, cotton, wool, and indigo.

English Trade Laws

The English charged the colonists high shipping costs. England used the raw materials from the colonies to make manufactured goods and exported them to other countries for huge profits.

In 1663 a new trade law said everything the colonies imported had to first be shipped to England and taxed. This made money for England, but raised the price of imports in the colonies. Colonists claimed England was destroying their economy. Some colonists began to smuggle, or secretly import, goods. They also traded in foreign ports and allowed ships from other countries into their ports. Luckily for colonists, England was far away, so it was difficult for the English government to make sure laws were being followed.

QUICK CHECK

Make Generalizations **What happened after England imposed taxes on trade goods?**

▼ The busy port of Boston in the 1600s

131

B WORLD TRADE

In 1675 King Charles II formed a committee to oversee colonial trade. This committee was formed to make sure the colonists were following trade laws. Its members soon learned that Boston Harbor was crowded with Dutch ships and ships from other countries. The colonists were unlawfully trading with Europe, the Caribbean, and Africa. Many colonists in Massachusetts were upset by English trade laws. They did not want to follow laws they thought were harmful to the colony. New England's shipbuilding industry and economy grew as a result of this illegal trade with other countries. As one historian said:

❝. . . selfishness of the English [trade laws] was digging a [wedge] between the mother country and the colonists.❞

Triangular Trade

Ships on the **triangular trade** routes sold products and picked up cargo at each stop. This came to be known as the triangular trade because the routes formed triangles on the map. The triangular trade made many merchants rich, especially in the New England Colonies. Using their wealth, merchants in Northern cities began trading with the Southern Colonies, exchanging Northern fish, rum, and grain for Southern rice, tobacco, and indigo. The illustration on this page shows how the colonial trade routes formed triangles.

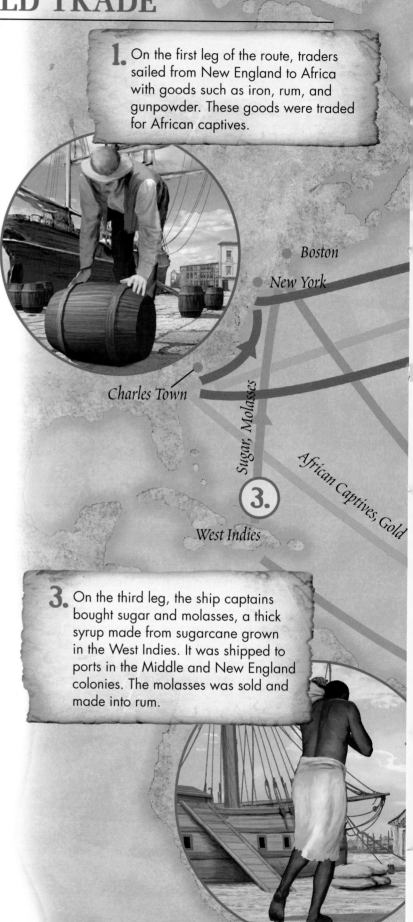

1. On the first leg of the route, traders sailed from New England to Africa with goods such as iron, rum, and gunpowder. These goods were traded for African captives.

Boston

New York

Charles Town

Sugar, Molasses

African Captives, Gold

3.

West Indies

3. On the third leg, the ship captains bought sugar and molasses, a thick syrup made from sugarcane grown in the West Indies. It was shipped to ports in the Middle and New England colonies. The molasses was sold and made into rum.

QUICK CHECK

Make Generalizations **Why did shipowners keep their ships filled with cargo on every leg of the voyage?**

The Triangular Trade

England

London

Lumber, Cod, Furs

Tobacco, Rice, Indigo

Manufactured Goods

Guns, Cloth

Africa

Rum, Iron

1.

2. African Captives

2. On the second leg of the route, the traders took the African captives to the West Indies. This part of the route was called the **Middle Passage**, because it was the middle part of the three-sided trade. In the West Indies, the Africans were sold into slavery.

Now that you have read about the triangular trade, let's find out what each region produced and exported. Each region's economy was based on its resources, industries, and the hard work of its people.

New England

Most of New England's soil was too rocky for farming. Many farmers there grew fruits and vegetables for themselves, but not enough to export. New Englanders needed other ways to earn a living. The forests provided lumber for the shipbuilding **industry**. An industry is all the businesses that make one kind of product or provide one kind of service. Wood was cheap in New England, where there was a good supply of trees. Logs were cut and tossed into rivers where they floated to towns and shipyards.

Soon Boston's shipbuilding industry competed with English shipbuilders. New Englanders also made excellent fishing boats, and fishing became a profitable industry. Cod was New England's "cash crop."

The Middle Colonies

Farmers in the Middle Colonies could supply just about everything needed for a picnic. They grew wheat for bread and raised dairy cattle for cheese. Farmers shipped these products to New York City and Philadelphia. From there they were exported to other countries. These port cities also became centers of business. Printers, shoemakers, cabinetmakers, and other craftworkers opened shops there.

DataGraphic
Major Colonial Exports

Most colonists made their living by farming. Each region grew different crops. Study the map and graph. Then answer the questions.

Major Exports, 1770

Value in British Pounds Sterling

Export	Value
Tobacco	900,000
Wheat	600,000
Fish	400,000
Rice	330,000
Indigo	130,000

Leading Colonial Exports, 1770

Exports of the 13 Colonies

New England Colonies

Middle Colonies

ATLANTIC OCEAN

Southern Colonies

Exports
- Fish
- Indigo
- Rice
- Tobacco
- Wheat

0   100 miles
0   100 kilometers

Think About Exports

1. What was New England's major export?

2. Which region's exports had the most value?

▲ Colonial general stores sold many of the manufactured goods people needed.

The Southern Colonies

The hot, humid climate and good soil of the Southern Colonies were well suited to growing crops. Tobacco and rice made many plantation owners wealthy in the Southern Colonies. At first these products were shipped only to England. Later they were shipped all over the world. Another crop grown in the Southern Colonies was indigo, a plant used to make blue dye. English merchants needed the blue dye from indigo for their huge cloth-making businesses. The tobacco, rice, and indigo trades brought great wealth to the Southern Colonies.

QUICK CHECK

Make Generalizations **Why did each region have a different economy?**

Check Understanding

1. **VOCABULARY** Draw a poster of triangular trade using the vocabulary terms below.

   triangular trade   **industry**
   Middle Passage

2. **READING SKILL** Make Generalizations
   Use your chart from page 130 to help you write a paragraph about colonial trade with England.

Text Clues	What You Know	Generalization

3. **Write About It** Write about why some colonists in New England settled in areas with heavy forests.

135

COLONIAL GOVERNMENTS

VOCABULARY

assembly p. 137

legislation p. 137

READING SKILL

Make Generalizations
Copy the chart below. As you read, fill it in to make a generalization about the power of colonial assemblies.

Text Clues	What You Know	Generalization

Illinois Learning Standards
16.B.2a (US), 16.D.2a (US), 18.B.2b

In 1699 the House of Burgesses moved from Jamestown to the new capital of Williamsburg, Virginia.

Visual Preview

How did values shape colonial governments?

A Charters allowed colonies to make their own laws and assemblies.

B Governors battled strong assemblies, which represented the people.

C The Zenger trial and Phyllis Wheatley's poems were calls for freedom.

SELF-GOVERNMENT

The colonists made many laws that were new ideas at the time. Colonists demanded rights that the English thought were almost rebellious! With laws protecting freedom of speech, colonists were building a system of government that represented the people.

An **assembly**, or lawmaking body, was guaranteed in the charters of most colonies. English kings allowed the colonies to make their own laws, but these laws had to be approved by England's government.

Colonial Assemblies

Sometimes assemblies made laws that protected and expanded people's rights and freedoms. Remember the Toleration Act in Maryland? Later, England would try to take some of these rights away.

The colonists felt independent from England, which was thousands of miles away. Colonial assemblies gathered to make laws for their colonies. This **legislation**, or making of laws, was a first step on the road to self-government.

Colonial governments weren't perfect. It fact, they were unfair to many groups. Women, indentured servants, enslaved Africans, and Native Americans could not vote or hold office. At first only white men who owned land could vote. Later a small number of men who did not own land were elected to assemblies. In some colonies, these voters also had to belong to a certain church.

QUICK CHECK

Make Generalizations Why were colonists on the road to self-government?

▼ A reenactment of the House of Burgesses during a recess

GOVERNORS AND GOVERNMENT

England allowed assemblies to control a colony's taxes and spending. This gave assemblies a great deal of power—the kind of power they held onto with a tight grip.

Powerful Assemblies

Colonists expected assemblies to represent their views rather than the views of the English rulers. Colonists saw themselves as English citizens who had the right to make their own decisions. The Virginia Charter stated that its colonists would have the same freedoms as people born in England.

Colonial governors constantly fought with their assemblies. Governors were usually appointed either by the king or by the colony's proprietor. Unlike the other colonies, Connecticut and Rhode Island elected their own governors. The governor's job was to represent the interests of the king or proprietor. The assembly's job was to represent the people of the colony. The governor could reject any law passed by a colonial assembly. The assemblies could stop paying the governor's expenses until their laws were approved. Withholding money wasn't the best way to solve a problem, but it helped assemblies protect their power.

Local Government

How did colonial towns solve their problems? In New England and some Middle Colonies, male colonists held town meetings. At these meetings, colonists sometimes had heated debates about local issues, elected local officials, and made laws. Most Southern

Colonies had county governments. Usually the governor appointed county officials. This gave more power to governors in the South.

Local courts settled disputes between individuals or answered questions about the law. Judges supervised colonial courts. The governor and the assembly selected colonists to serve as judges.

Natural Rights

John Locke believed that people were naturally good. He was an English thinker who believed that all people have "natural rights." Among these rights were life, freedom, and the right to own property. Locke wrote that the main duty of government was to protect these rights. When a government failed to protect these rights, Locke thought people could overthrow, or change, that government. Most colonists understood what Locke meant by life and property rights. But people disagreed about the meaning of the word *freedom*.

QUICK CHECK

Make Generalizations **Generalize Locke's belief about what people should do if a government fails to protect their natural rights.**

◀ A lawbreaker might have to spend days in the public pillory. This form of public embarrassment was a punishment for minor crimes, such as swearing. More serious crimes, such as robbery, could be punished by whipping or even hanging.

Citizenship
Express Your Opinion

How can expressing your opinion bring change? Many colonists had heated debates about local issues. By expressing their opinions they had a voice in the decisions that affected their lives. Voting is one way to express your opinion. Another way is by writing to your mayor, governor, or member of Congress about issues you care about. You can also write an editorial for your local newspaper or Web site. Expressing an opinion is a right all American citizens enjoy.

▲ **Write About It** John Locke believed people were naturally good. Write an essay about why you agree or disagree with Locke. Use examples to support your opinion.

Does freedom include printing something bad about someone, even if it is true? John Peter Zenger came from Germany and started a newspaper in New York City called *The New York Weekly Journal*. In the newspaper, Zenger published articles about the governor of New York, William Cosby. Cosby took Zenger to court, saying that Zenger's articles had insulted him. Zenger's lawyer, Andrew Hamilton, told the jury that Zenger had the right to print the truth. Read a section from Hamilton's address on this page.

Hamilton's words meant that people had the freedom to write or speak the truth. The jury agreed and found Zenger not guilty. The Zenger trial helped establish the idea that newspaper publishers could not be punished for printing the truth. Later, freedom of the press became part of the U.S. Constitution.

Primary Sources

"The question before the court and you . . . is the best cause. It is the cause of liberty. . . . [E]very man who prefers freedom to a life of slavery will bless and honor you. . . . [We] have laid a noble foundation for securing to ourselves, our **posterity**, and our neighbors . . . the liberty both of exposing and opposing **arbitrary** power (in these parts of the world, at least) by speaking and writing the truth. . . ."

A section from Address to the Jury by Andrew Hamilton August 14, 1735

posterity   future generations
arbitrary   not limited

▼ Andrew Hamilton defending John Peter Zenger during his trial.

Write About It Write about how freedom of speech can expose dishonesty in elected officials.

Phillis Wheatley

Some enslaved Africans also wrote about freedom. Phillis Wheatley published her first poem at age 13. Wheatley believed enslaved Africans had natural rights. In one of her poems, Phillis Wheatley urged colonists to fight for freedom:

"No longer shalt [you fear] the iron chain . . . meant t'enslave the land."

George Washington praised Wheatley's writing. While growing up, her life had been difficult. At age seven Wheatley was kidnapped from Africa and enslaved. Then she was purchased in Boston by John Wheatley, but her life was different from most enslaved Africans. John's wife, Susannah Wheatley, taught Phillis to read and write English and other languages. By the time she was 13 years old, she was writing poetry. In 1773, at age 20, Phillis Wheatley published a book of poems and was freed from slavery.

QUICK CHECK

Make Generalizations How was Phillis Wheatley's life different from most enslaved Africans?

John Peter Zenger

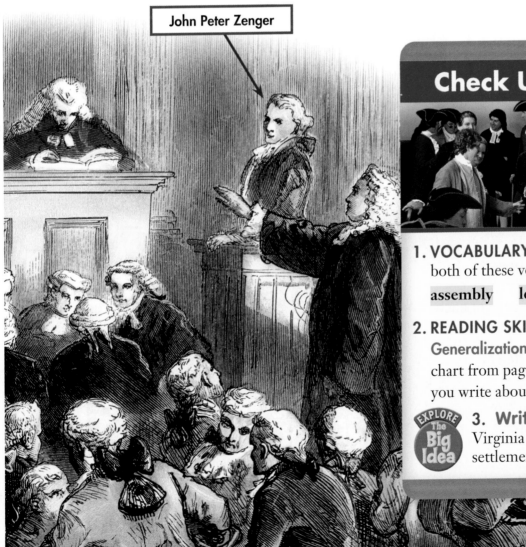

Check Understanding

1. **VOCABULARY** Write one sentence using both of these vocabulary words.

   assembly   **legislation**

2. **READING SKILL Make Generalizations** Use your chart from page 136 to help you write about colonial assemblies.

Text Clues	What You Know	Generalization

3. **Write About It** How did the Virginia Charter encourage settlement?

Vocabulary

Number a paper from 1 to 4. Beside each number write the word from the list below that matches the description.

apprentice   slave codes

industry   assembly

1. Businesses that provide one kind of product or service

2. Rules that controlled the lives of enslaved Africans

3. A lawmaking body

4. A person who works for a skilled person to learn a craft or trade

Comprehension and Critical Thinking

5. How did the economy of the Southern Colonies contribute to the growth of slavery?

6. **Reading Skill** Why did some Puritans leave Massachusetts Bay Colony to start other colonies?

7. **Critical Thinking** Why did William Penn want freedom of religion in Pennsylvania?

8. **Critical Thinking** Why did England allow colonies to have assemblies?

Skill

Use Historical Maps

Write a complete sentence to answer each question.

9. Which main groups settled in Pennsylvania?

10. Which main group settled in Northwestern Maryland?

Main Immigrant Groups in 1760

Legend:
- African
- Dutch
- English
- German
- Scotch-Irish
- No main group
- — Colony boundary

0   50   100 miles
0   50   100 kilometers

NEW YORK   MA

CT

New York

PA

Philadelphia

NEW JERSEY

Baltimore

DELAWARE

MARYLAND

VIRGINIA

ATLANTIC OCEAN

Illinois Standards Achievement Test Preparation

"The question before the court and you . . . is the best cause. It is the cause of liberty . . . [and] every man who prefers freedom to a life of slavery will bless and honor you. . . . [We] have laid a noble foundation for securing to ourselves, our posterity, and our neighbors . . . the liberty both of exposing and opposing arbitrary power (in these parts of the world, at least) by speaking and writing the truth. . . ."

A section from the Address to the Jury

by Andrew Hamilton August 14, 1735

1

According to Andrew Hamilton, what is the best cause?

Ⓐ Liberty
Ⓑ Slavery
Ⓒ Power
Ⓓ Security

3

Based on the information from this passage, who is Hamilton speaking to?

Ⓐ Judge
Ⓑ Lawyers
Ⓒ Jury
Ⓓ Court reporter

2

Which of the following could replace the word *posterity* in the above sentence?

Ⓐ Government officials
Ⓑ Farmland
Ⓒ Future generations
Ⓓ Writing

4

What does Hamilton think will expose and oppose "arbitrary power"?

Ⓐ With ears
Ⓑ By feeling
Ⓒ By tasting
Ⓓ By smelling

Activities

Why do people settle new areas?

Write About the Big Idea

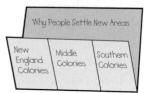

FOLDABLES™
Study Organizer

Descriptive Journal Entry
Use the Unit 3 Foldable to help you write a descriptive journal entry that answers the Big Idea question, *Why do people settle new areas?* Use the notes you wrote under each tab for details to support each main idea. Be sure to describe the region and why people settled in that area.

Make a Bar Graph

With a partner, make two bar graphs showing the population growth of the Thirteen Colonies from 1700 to 1760 and the projected population of the United States from 2000 to 2060.

1. Use these figures to make your colonial bar graph.

1700	250,900	1740	905,600
1720	466,200	1760	1,593,600

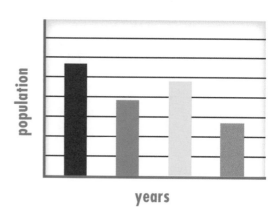

2. Use these figures to make your U.S. bar graph.

2000	275 million	2040	370 million
2020	323 million	2060	432 million

When you have finished your bar graphs, take turns presenting each graph to the class. Compare and contrast the rate of population growth.

The Struggle for
North
America

Unit 4

Essential Question
Why do people take risks?

EXPLORE The Big Idea

FOLDABLES™ Study Organizer

Main Idea and Details
Make and label a Concept map before you read this unit. Write the word **Risks** at the top. Label the three tabs **French, British,** and **American**. Use the Foldable to organize information.

Risks

French | British | American

LOG ON
For more about Unit 4 go to
www.macmillanmh.com

British General Braddock was fatally wounded during the French and Indian War.

PEOPLE, PLACES, AND EVENTS

Robert Cavelier, Sieur de La Salle

Jean Baptiste Le Moyne, Sieur de Bienville

Mississippi River

1682
La Salle claims Mississippi River for France

New Orleans

1718
Bienville founds New Orleans

1675   1700   1725

La Salle led French explorers down the **Mississippi River** by canoe in search of a water route across North America.

Today the Mississippi River is one of the world's most important waterways.

Bienville believed it was important for the French to build cities in Louisiana. He founded **New Orleans**.

Today you can visit cities founded by the French, including New Orleans and Baton Rouge.

Thomas Jefferson

George Washington

Philadelphia

1776
Jefferson writes
the Declaration of
Independence

Yorktown

1781
British surrender to
George Washington
at Yorktown, Virginia

1750   1775   1800

Thomas Jefferson wrote the Declaration
of Independence at the Graff House in
Philadelphia.

Today you can tour the rebuilt Graff House in
Philadelphia.

The British surrendered to **George
Washington** at **Yorktown**.

Today you can see the battlefield where the
fighting of the American Revolution ended.

147

Lesson 1

VOCABULARY

tributary p. 149

territory p. 149

READING SKILL

Main Idea and Details

Copy the chart below. Use it to fill in the main idea and details about the French exploration of the Mississippi River valley.

Main Idea	Details

Illinois Learning Standards

16.D.2a (US), 17.C.2a, 17.C.2b, 17.D.2b

The French in Louisiana

French explorers paddled canoes from the Great Lakes to the mouth of the Mississippi River.

Visual Preview

How did France's control of the Mississippi River affect settlement?

A La Salle claimed new territory for France and named it Louisiana.

B French settlers built settlements at Biloxi Bay and New Orleans.

A   LA SALLE CLAIMS LOUISIANA

In 1670 New France consisted of only a few fur trading posts in Canada. This would change after 1673, when two French explorers reached a mighty river flowing south. Native Americans called it the Mississippi—"Father of Waters."

The first French colonists to explore the Mississippi River were Jacques Marquette, a missionary, and Louis Jolliet, a fur trader. In 1673 they traveled by canoe as far as the Arkansas River, a **tributary** of the Mississippi, before turning back. A tributary is a river or stream that flows into a larger river.

La Salle's Expedition

As word of the enormous river spread across New France, other explorers saw an opportunity to gain wealth. In 1682 Robert de La Salle led an expedition down the Mississippi River. His followers built a fort at what is today Memphis, Tennessee. Then they continued, paddling to the mouth of the river on the Gulf of Mexico. There La Salle claimed the Mississippi River and its tributaries for France. He named the **territory** Louisiana. A territory is an area of land controlled by another country.

Plan for Settlement

Excited by his discovery, La Salle sailed to France to gather support for a new colony. Two years later, he returned with several hundred men. The plan was to sail west across the Gulf of Mexico and build a settlement at the mouth of the Mississippi River. From there, La Salle planned to travel farther west and take control of silver mines in New Spain.

La Salle's plan excited his followers, but it ended in failure. A poor navigator, he sailed 400 miles past the mouth of the river, landing in present-day Texas. Many of La Salle's men died from disease and starvation. Still others were killed by Native Americans. In the end, the few men who survived revolted against La Salle. He was killed by his own men.

QUICK CHECK

Main Idea and Details What happened on La Salle's second expedition to the mouth of the Mississippi River?

EVENT

On April 9, 1682, Robert de La Salle **claimed the Louisiana Territory** for France. He named the territory for the French king, Louis XIV.

Louisiana Territory claimed

B SETTLING LOUISIANA

By 1690 France had claimed much of what is now the central United States and Canada. At that time only a few thousand settlers lived in New France. Almost no Europeans had settled in the Louisiana Territory.

The French realized that they were in danger of losing Louisiana to England or to Spain, whose explorers had reached the area. King Louis XIV of France decided to strengthen French control of the region.

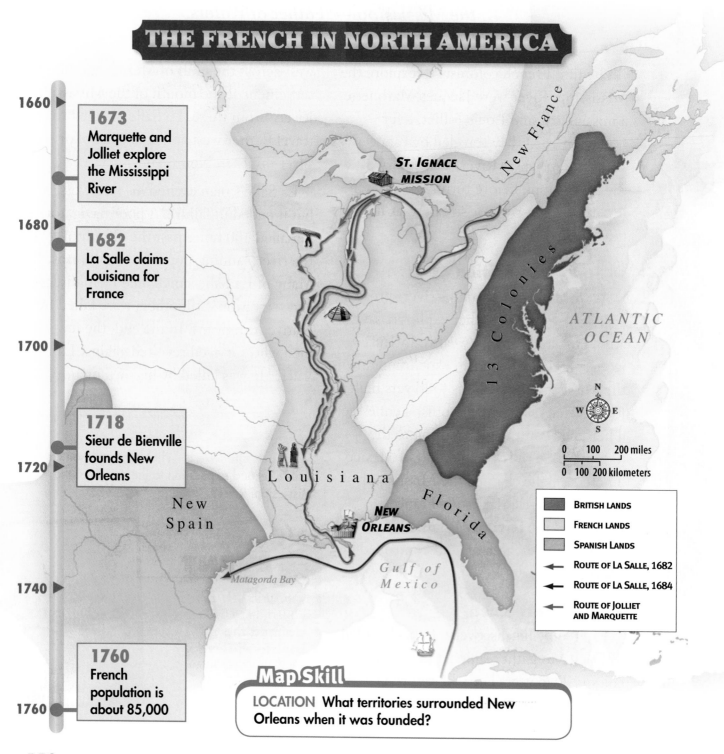

THE FRENCH IN NORTH AMERICA

1660

1673
Marquette and Jolliet explore the Mississippi River

1680

1682
La Salle claims Louisiana for France

1700

1718
Sieur de Bienville founds New Orleans

1720

1740

1760
French population is about 85,000

1760

ST. IGNACE MISSION

New France

13 Colonies

ATLANTIC OCEAN

Louisiana

New Spain

Florida

NEW ORLEANS

Gulf of Mexico

Matagorda Bay

N W E S

0   100   200 miles
0   100 200 kilometers

BRITISH LANDS
FRENCH LANDS
SPANISH LANDS
ROUTE OF LA SALLE, 1682
ROUTE OF LA SALLE, 1684
ROUTE OF JOLLIET AND MARQUETTE

Map Skill

LOCATION What territories surrounded New Orleans when it was founded?

The city of New Orleans was settled about 100 miles north of the mouth of the Mississippi River.

First Settlements

In 1698 the French king appointed Pierre Le Moyne, Sieur d'Iberville as the first governor of Louisiana. D'Iberville agreed with the king—France needed to control the Mississippi River. To do that, France needed a larger population in the area. D'Iberville feared the English would take over and wrote:

"If France does not seize this most beautiful part of America and set up a colony . . . "

New Orleans

After d'Iberville died in 1706, his brother Jean-Baptiste Le Moyne, Sieur de Bienville became governor of Louisiana. In 1718 he founded New Orleans about 100 miles north of the mouth of the Mississippi River. The settlement drew many settlers to Louisiana.

New Orleans became the largest French settlement in Louisiana. Unlike settlers of New France, who worked mainly in the fur trade, colonists in Louisiana built plantations. Planters brought in enslaved Africans to raise indigo, rice, and tobacco.

Slow Growth

By 1740 France claimed an area from Canada down the Mississippi River to the Gulf of Mexico. By 1760 the French had 85,000 settlers, compared to 2 million in the English colonies. However, French control of the area prevented the English from moving west.

QUICK CHECK

Main Idea and Details **In what ways were settlers in Louisiana different from settlers in New France?**

Check Understanding

1. **VOCABULARY** Write two sentences about Louisiana that use these vocabulary words.

   tributary   territory

2. **READING SKILL Main Idea and Details.** Use the chart from page 148 to explain how New Orleans was founded.

Main Idea	Details

3. **Write About It** What made La Salle take the risk of sailing from France around Florida to the mouth of the Mississippi River?

The French and Indian War

Lesson 2

VOCABULARY

French and Indian War p. 153

Treaty of Paris p. 154

Proclamation of 1763 p. 154

READING SKILL

Main Idea and Details
Copy the chart. Use it to list the main idea and details about the French and Indian War.

Main Idea	Details

Illinois Learning Standards
16.B.2b (US), 17.C.2b, 17.D.2b

French officers meet leaders of the Wyandot, also called the Huron.

Visual Preview

How did the French and Indian War change the colonies?

A English settlers moved to land claimed by France.

B Great Britain's victory united English colonists for the first time as Americans.

A WAR IN NORTH AMERICA

In 1707 the king of England united England and Scotland and named the new country Great Britain. Its people were now known as "British." British settlers fought the French over land in North America.

Disagreements between France and Great Britain arose when English colonists settled on land claimed by France in the Ohio River Valley. The settlers were farmers. The French trappers feared that the newcomers would cut down forests, which would hurt their fur trade. The dispute over land led to the **French and Indian War**. In this war, the French and their Native American allies, the Wyandot, fought the British.

Washington's Victory

In 1754 the lieutenant governor of Virginia sent a young officer, George Washington, to Fort Duquesne, located in present-day Pittsburgh, Pennsylvania. Washington's men defeated a force of French soldiers near the fort. It was the first battle of the French and Indian War. But Washington did not capture the fort.

Loss for Great Britain

In 1755 British General Edward Braddock led British troops against Fort Duquesne. Washington was one of his officers. This time the British were defeated. Nearly 900 British troops were killed or wounded by the French and Wyandot. Braddock was killed.

Washington later wrote:

> "I luckily escaped . . . though I had four bullets through my coat, and two horses shot out under me."

The Turning Point

News of the French victory caused panic among the British colonists. They asked British leader William Pitt to spend more money in the war. In November 1758, with Pitt's support, the British captured Fort Duquesne. They renamed it Fort Pitt. What city still bears his name?

QUICK CHECK

Main Idea and Details. **Why did French trappers want to keep British settlers out of the Ohio River Valley?**

▼ British and French troops also fought in Canada during the French and Indian War.

THE WAR ENDS

After the victory at Fort Duquesne, the British decided to drive the French out of Canada. In June 1759 British forces attacked Quebec, which is located on steep cliffs above the St. Lawrence River. To carry out this surprise attack, British troops silently climbed narrow paths up the cliffs at night.

The French awoke to find the British at the gates of the city. The siege lasted for months. Finally, on September 13, the French surrendered Quebec. One year later, the British seized Montreal, and the French were forced from Canada.

The Proclamation of 1763

War between Great Britain and France in Canada ended with the fall of Montreal. But battles between the two countries continued in Europe until 1763, when France was defeated. The two countries signed the **Treaty of Paris**, ending the French and Indian War. After the treaty was signed, Great Britain claimed all of France's colonies in North America.

After the war, the French could no longer help the Native Americans. On the other hand, Great Britain could not afford to use troops to protect settlers in the Ohio Valley. As a result, Great Britain issued the **Proclamation of 1763**. This official announcement set aside land west of the Appalachian Mountains for Native American groups.

North America, 1763

Hudson Bay

Great Lakes

St. Lawrence River

THE THIRTEEN COLONIES

Mississippi

LOUISIANA

PACIFIC OCEAN

NEW SPAIN

Rio Grande

ATLANTIC OCEAN

FLORIDA

Gulf of Mexico

West Indies

Caribbean Sea

N W E S

- British lands
- French lands
- Spanish lands
- Russian lands
- Disputed or unclaimed lands by Europeans
— Proclamation Line of 1763

0   500   1,000 miles
0   500   1,000 kilometers

Map Skill

LOCATION Why was land under Spanish control called Louisiana?

Pontiac

Although the British claimed former French lands, they did not have firm control of them. In 1763 Ottawa Chief Pontiac united Native Americans in the Ohio River valley to drive out the British. He called the British:

> Those who will do you nothing but harm.

▼ British troops climbed the steep cliffs below Quebec and attacked French troops in the city.

Pontiac's fighters captured and burned several British settlements in the area but were defeated by the British army in 1763.

Results of the War

The British victory in the French and Indian War united the colonists. They had joined together to fight a powerful enemy. They had discovered strong leaders such as Washington. Soon a new, independent spirit developed among the "Americans," as they called themselves. Victory in the French and Indian War set the stage for the American Revolution.

QUICK CHECK

Main Idea and Details **What was the purpose of the Proclamation of 1763?**

Check Understanding

1. **VOCABULARY** Make a time line of the French and Indian War. Use the terms below.

   French and Indian War   **Treaty of Paris**

   Proclamation of 1763

2. **READING SKILL** Main Idea and Details Use the graphic organizer to help write two paragraphs about the French and Indian War.

Main Idea	Details

3. **Write About It** Explain the risks that British settlers took when they moved to the Ohio River Valley.

155

VOCABULARY

Stamp Act p. 157

boycott p. 157

repeal p. 157

delegates p. 159

READING SKILL

Main Idea and Details

Copy the chart below. Use it to fill out the main idea and details of the colonial protests against Great Britain.

Main Idea	Details

Illinois Learning Standards

14.D.2, 16.B.2b (US)

COLONISTS PROTEST BRITISH RULE

Colonists burned printed documents and British stamps to protest the Stamp Act.

Visual Preview

What caused the colonists to unite against Great Britain?

A The colonists protested the taxes British leaders raised to pay war debts.

B British troops came to Boston and other cities to stop protests.

NEW TAXES

An angry crowd marched down the narrow streets of Boston protesting the newly passed Stamp Act. Why were they so angry about stamps?

The French and Indian War was very costly for the British government. In 1763 King George III and British leaders agreed that taxes should be raised to pay the war debts. But British citizens were already paying high taxes. So British leaders decided to raise taxes on the colonists.

◀ A British stamp used on printed documents

The Stamp Act

In 1765 the British government passed the **Stamp Act**. Under this act, colonists had to buy stamps and place them on all printed documents, including letters, wills, newspapers, and even playing cards.

Many colonists said the British could not tax them without their consent, or agreement. One colonist who led the fight against the Stamp Act was Samuel Adams of Massachusetts. He sent protest letters to newspapers. In one letter he wrote:

❝ If our trade may be taxed, why not our lands? Why not . . . everything we possess or use? ❞

Colonists Organize

When the Stamp Act went into effect on November 1, angry colonists staged a **boycott**. To boycott means to refuse to buy goods or services from a person, group, or country. Most colonists refused to use the stamps. To protest the Stamp Act, Adams and other colonists formed a group they called the Sons of Liberty.

In 1766 Parliament voted to **repeal**, or end, the Stamp Act. However, in 1767 Parliament passed the Townshend Acts. They taxed factory-made goods such as paper, glass, and paint.

Again, the colonists boycotted the newly taxed items. They also boycotted any colonial merchant who sold or used taxed goods. British leaders feared that the boycotts could lead to violence. They sent troops to the city of Boston, whose citizens had caused the most trouble.

QUICK CHECK

Main Idea and Details How did British leaders raise taxes on the colonies?

▲ Silversmith Paul Revere made this engraving of the Boston Massacre.

Engrav'd Printed & Sold by PAUL REVERE BOSTON

B PROTEST IN BOSTON

No city in the colonies caused more problems for the British than Boston, Massachusetts. It was the location of two key events that led to the Revolution.

The Boston Massacre

On March 6, 1770, colonists gathered at the Boston Customs House, where taxes on goods from Great Britain were paid. The group included Crispus Attucks, a person who had escaped from slavery. Historians are uncertain exactly what happened next.

It seems that a member of the crowd insulted a British soldier, who knocked the boy down. Other colonists threw snowballs at the guard. British soldiers fired into the crowd, killing five colonists, including Attucks. This event became known as the Boston Massacre.

The Boston Tea Party

The British government repealed the Townshend Acts, but it passed the Tea Act in 1773. This act was passed to help the British East India Company. Parliament allowed the British East India Company to sell tea in the colonies without paying import taxes. Instead a tax was placed on colonists who bought tea. The tax was low, but colonists were angered that another law had been passed without their consent or approval.

In November 1773 three British East India Company ships entered Boston Harbor. Colonists refused to allow the ships to unload. The governor of Massachusetts, Thomas Hutchinson, ordered the ships to stay in the harbor until the tea was sold.

On the night of December 16, 1773, about 50 Sons of Liberty, some disguised as Mohawk Indians, boarded the ships. They broke open the tea chests and emptied them into the harbor. Similar attacks took place in Annapolis, Maryland, and New York city. However, this event became known as the Boston Tea Party.

The British Parliament responded by closing Boston Harbor until the colonists paid for the tea. Town meetings were banned. More British soldiers were sent to the colonies. Colonists called Parliament's actions "The Intolerable Acts." Intolerable means unbearable. The Intolerable Acts united the colonies against Great Britain. **Delegates** from the colonies met in Philadelphia to discuss the problem. Delegates are people who are chosen to represent other people. The delegates formed the First Continental Congress to decide what action to take against Great Britain.

QUICK CHECK

Main Idea and Details **Why did the Intolerable Acts cause problems between the colonies and Great Britain?**

▼ Colonists disguised as Mohawk Indians threw British tea into Boston Harbor.

Check Understanding

1. **VOCABULARY** Write three sentences using two of the words below.

   Stamp Act   **repeal**

   boycott   **delegate**

2. **READING SKILL** Main Idea and Details Use the chart from page 156 to write a paragraph about disagreements over taxes that led to protests in the colonies.

Main Idea	Details

3. **Write About It** Why were colonists willing to take risks by protesting British laws?

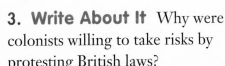

Lesson 4

VOCABULARY

militia p. 161

ammunition p. 163

READING SKILL

Main Idea and Details

Copy the chart below. Use it to fill in the main idea and details of the first battles of the Revolution.

Main Idea	Details

Illinois Learning Standards

16.A.2b, 16.B.2b (US)

THE REVOLUTION BEGINS

Minutemen fought off an attack by British soldiers at the Old North Bridge in Concord, Massachusetts.

Visual Preview

What caused the American Revolution?

A The first shots were fired at Lexington and Concord.

B Colonists took over Fort Ticonderoga but lost at the Battle of Bunker Hill.

C By 1776 the British left Boston, but most colonists felt independent.

LEXINGTON AND CONCORD

By 1775 colonists had stored weapons in Lexington and Concord, near Boston. Two well-known supporters of independence, Samuel Adams and John Hancock, were also in Lexington.

On April 18, 1775, British general Thomas Gage sent about 700 soldiers from Boston. They had orders to seize the weapons and arrest Samuel Adams and John Hancock.

Paul Revere, a Boston silversmith, set off for Lexington to warn of the British approach. A second rider, William Dawes, took a different route. A third rider, Dr. Samuel Prescott, also joined them.

By the time the British reached Lexington, Adams and Hancock had fled. Captain John Parker waited with colonial **militia**, called minutemen. Militia are volunteer soldiers who fight only in an emergency.

The First Shots

No one knows who fired first, but many shots rang out. Eight militia members were killed. British troops continued toward Concord, about ten miles away.

When the British soldiers arrived, many minutemen were waiting. They stopped the British there. As the British retreated to Boston, minutemen continued shooting along the way. More than 90 British soldiers were killed.

QUICK CHECK

Main Idea and Details **What did British troops do on April 18, 1775?**

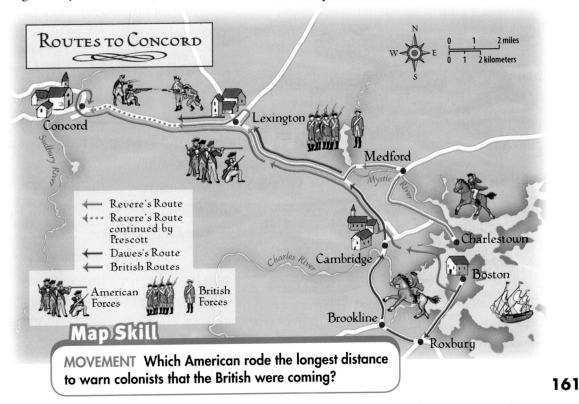

ROUTES TO CONCORD

Concord · Lexington · Medford · Charlestown · Cambridge · Boston · Brookline · Roxbury

Sudbury River · *Mystic River* · *Charles River*

← Revere's Route
⋯ Revere's Route continued by Prescott
← Dawes's Route
← British Routes

American Forces · British Forces

Map Skill

MOVEMENT **Which American rode the longest distance to warn colonists that the British were coming?**

This famous painting shows colonists fighting British soldiers at the Battle of Bunker Hill.

B EARLY BATTLES

Three weeks after the battles took place in Massachusetts, a young New Englander named Benedict Arnold led a militia force toward Fort Ticonderoga. This was a British fort on Lake Champlain in New York. News traveled slowly in the 1700s. Therefore, the British at Fort Ticonderoga did not know about the events at Lexington and Concord.

Ethan Allen

Arnold planned to capture the cannons at Fort Ticonderoga and take them to the colonial army camped near Boston. His force joined those of another New Englander— Ethan Allen. Allen's troops, the Green Mountain Boys, were militia from the area that is now Vermont.

Early on May 10, 1775, Allen's men sneaked into Fort Ticonderoga. They surprised the guards, capturing the fort without firing a shot.

The Battle of Bunker Hill

In June, back in Boston, British general Thomas Gage decided to take control of the hills around Boston. That way, American cannons could not fire down into the city. But colonists learned of the plan. The colonial militia, led by Colonel William Prescott and General Israel Putnam, were ordered to defend Bunker Hill in Charlestown across the Charles River from Boston. Instead, they decided to defend Breed's Hill, which was closer to the river. The colonists worked all night to build earthen walls for protection.

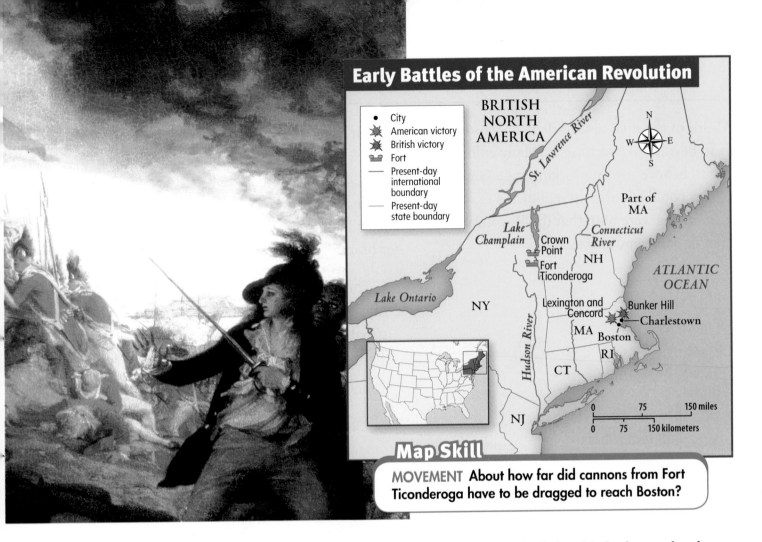

Early Battles of the American Revolution

Legend:
- City
- American victory
- British victory
- Fort
- Present-day international boundary
- Present-day state boundary

BRITISH NORTH AMERICA

St. Lawrence River

Lake Champlain
Crown Point
Fort Ticonderoga

Lake Ontario

NY

Hudson River

Part of MA

Connecticut River

NH

Lexington and Concord

MA

Boston

Bunker Hill
Charlestown

ATLANTIC OCEAN

RI

CT

NJ

0   75   150 miles
0   75   150 kilometers

Map Skill

MOVEMENT About how far did cannons from Fort Ticonderoga have to be dragged to reach Boston?

The Battle Begins

On June 17, British soldiers led by Major John Pitcairn crossed the Charles River in boats. They marched up Breed's Hill toward the earthen walls where colonists waited. The Americans did not have much **ammunition**, or musket balls and gunpowder. Officers told them not to waste ammunition by firing at soldiers too far away. Historians say that either Prescott or Putnam said:

> **❝**Don't shoot until you see the whites of their eyes.**❞**

A British Victory

Twice the British charged up the hill. Both times they were turned back by American fire. Finally the Americans ran out of powder and musket balls. Peter Brown, an American soldier, described the third advance by the British troops:

> **❝**When the enemy came in, [I] jumped over the wall and ran . . . [musket] balls flew like hail stones and cannon[s] roared like thunder. . . .**❞**

The British won what was later called the Battle of Bunker Hill. More than 400 colonists were killed or wounded, but the victory was costly for the British. More than 1,000 British soldiers were killed or wounded. The British commander, Major Pitcairn, was one of many British officers killed that day.

QUICK CHECK

Main Idea and Details. What happened at the Battle of Bunker Hill?

NEW YEAR BRINGS HOPE

Word of the high cost of British victories spread beyond Massachusetts. Many colonists came to believe that by working together, the colonies could win their freedom. As 1776 began, hopes were high that the Revolution would be short and successful.

The British Leave Boston

Many colonists even found hope in the defeat at Bunker Hill. The British had won, but the Americans had fought hard. Abigail Adams had watched the battle from a hill near her house. She wrote to her husband, John:

> **"The spirits of the people are very good. The loss of Charlestown affects them no more than a drop in the bucket. . . ."**

Colonial soldiers led by General Henry Knox dragged cannons from Fort Ticonderoga to Boston.

In January 1776 cannons dragged from Fort Ticonderoga and Crown Point by colonial soldiers finally reached Boston. Soon, cannon fire poured into British camps in the city. In March, the British sailed out of Boston.

Some Seek Compromise

As American colonists heard about these battles they had to make a choice. Should they join the rebels or remain loyal to Britain? Most colonists wanted to end what they saw as British bullying. But not all colonists wanted to completely cut ties with Great Britain. They hoped that the British government would compromise. Some of these colonists worked to help the British government. Others feared that they might lose their property during the fighting. Still others, called Loyalists, simply did not want to separate from Great Britain. They thought that taxes and restrictions were not good reasons for rebellion.

No Turning Back

Most colonists understood that a compromise would not be reached. They knew that once British soldiers were killed, the British government would not back down. But the events around Boston made colonists see themselves in a new way. They were no longer British citizens living in British colonies. They were citizens of a new country that was fighting to free itself from British rule. Patrick Henry declared this at the First Continental Congress:

"I am not a Virginian but an American."

QUICK CHECK

Main Idea and Details Why did some colonists want to compromise with Great Britain?

▼ Cannons like this were dragged from Fort Ticonderoga to Boston.

Check Understanding

1. **VOCABULARY** Write one sentence using both vocabulary words below.

   militia ammunition

2. **READING SKILL** Main Idea and Details Use the chart from page 160 to write a paragraph explaining why colonists saw hope in the defeat at Bunker Hill.

Main Idea	Details

EXPLORE The Big Idea

3. **Write About It** In what ways did the events of 1775 and 1776 show colonists the risks they were taking by fighting the British?

The Declaration of Independence

Lesson 5

VOCABULARY

Continental Army p. 167

Declaration of Independence p. 168

READING SKILL

Main Idea and Details
Copy the chart below. Use it to fill in the main idea and details of the Declaration of Independence.

Main Idea	Details

Illinois Learning Standards
14.A.2, 14.F.2, 16.B.2b (US), 16.B.2b (W)

Delegates to the Second Continental Congress signed the Declaration of Independence in 1776.

Visual Preview

Why is the Second Continental Congress important?

A The Congress sent a peace petition to Great Britain that King George III rejected.

B The Congress approved the Declaration of Independence.

PEACE PLANS FAIL

On May 10, 1775, about a month after the battles at Lexington and Concord, colonial delegates met in Philadelphia at the Second Continental Congress.

John Hancock, a Boston merchant who had escaped from Lexington, was elected president of the Second Continental Congress. Hancock soon learned that the delegates did not all have the same goals for the Congress.

Delegates Disagree

Samuel Adams and John Adams, from Massachusetts, and Richard Henry Lee and Thomas Jefferson, of Virginia, wanted independence from Great Britain. John Dickinson of Pennsylvania and others hoped the colonies could remain British subjects but could govern themselves.

In July 1775 the Congress sent what they called the "Olive Branch Petition" to King George III. An olive branch is a symbol of peace. The petition asked the king to repeal his governing policies for the colonies. The petition angered the king. He refused to even read it. Instead he ordered more troops to be sent to the colonies. When word of the king's response reached the Congress, most delegates agreed that independence was their only choice.

A Continental Army

By late 1775, the Congress faced the task of raising an army and naming a commander. Most fighting had taken place in the North. This led John Adams to say that a Southern commander would help unite the regions. He nominated George Washington from Virginia as the leader of the

King George III ▶

Continental Army, the name given to the colonial force. Washington had served as an officer in the French and Indian War, and colonial soldiers trusted him.

Congress sent Representatives to France, the Netherlands, and Spain to seek financial support. These countries wanted to help the Americans fight Great Britain, their longtime enemy. However, Great Britain was the strongest country in Europe. No country would risk sending money or supplies until the Continental Army proved it could defeat the British.

QUICK CHECK

Main Idea and Details How did George Washington become the leader of the Continental Army?

THE DECLARATION OF INDEPENDENCE

In June 1776 a committee was appointed by Congress to write a **Declaration of Independence**, a document stating that the colonies were independent from Great Britain. The committee members were John Adams of Massachusetts, Benjamin Franklin of Pennsylvania, Robert Livingston of New York, Roger Sherman of Connecticut, and Thomas Jefferson of Virginia. The members of the committee decided that Jefferson should write the first draft.

Writing Begins

Jefferson worked on a draft for two weeks. Then Franklin and Adams made some changes and presented the draft to the Congress on June 28. Throughout the hot summer days of early July, delegates discussed the final wording of the Declaration. Adams later said he was delighted with Jefferson's "high tone," yet he later wrote:

> **"There were other expressions . . . which I thought too much like scolding."**

Jefferson included a list of crimes that he accused the king of committing. Other delegates wanted to remove parts of this section before sending it to the king.

Jefferson had also attacked the slave trade. Representatives from the Southern colonies, whose economy depended on slavery, removed words attacking slavery and the slave trade.

General Washington had the Declaration of Independence read to his soldiers.

The power of Jefferson's words inspired the delegates. But the final statement of his document made the most important point:

> **"The good people of these colonies, solemnly publish and declare, that these United Colonies are, and of right ought to be free and independent states."**

Approval and Signing

At last the delegates were satisfied. They passed the final version of the Declaration of Independence on July 4, 1776. John Hancock, as president, signed it first. He said that he wrote his name large enough for the king to read without his glasses. Americans still celebrate this date as "Independence Day."

Soon copies of the Declaration were sent throughout the colonies. On July 19 Congress ordered a special copy of the Declaration to be written on parchment, a sheepskin paper used for important documents. Its new title was "The Unanimous Declaration of the Thirteen United States of America." It was the first time the name of the new country was used in an official document.

On August 2, the other delegates added their signatures under Hancock's, which was the largest. Eventually, 56 delegates signed the document. Every person who signed it became an enemy of the king and could be hanged. Declaring independence was a great risk.

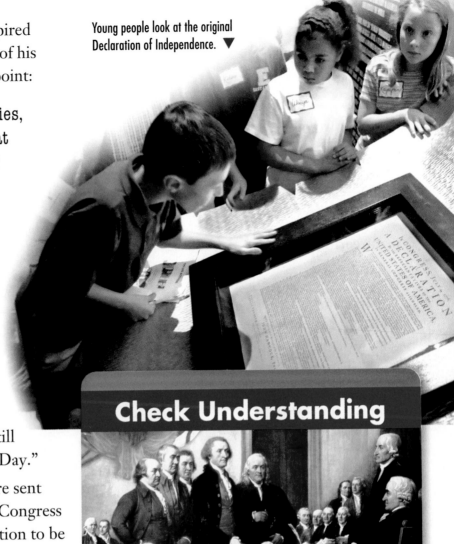

Young people look at the original Declaration of Independence. ▼

Check Understanding

1. **VOCABULARY** Write a sentence explaining how the Second Continental Congress is connected to each vocabulary term.

   Continental army

   Declaration of Independence

2. **READING SKILL** Main Idea and Details Use the chart from page 166 to explain how the Declaration of Independence was written.

Main Idea	Details

3. **Write About It** Why did King George's rejection of the Olive Branch Petition cause the colonists to risk their lives for independence?

QUICK CHECK

Main Idea and Details **What was the purpose of the Declaration of Independence?**

Fighting the War

VOCABULARY

Patriot p. 171

mercenary p. 172

Loyalist p. 172

profiteering p. 176

inflation p. 176

READING SKILL

Main Idea and Details
Copy the chart below. Use it to fill in the main idea and details about the ways colonists supported the war.

Main Idea	Details

Illinois Learning Standards
14.F.2, 16.B.2b (US), 18.A.2

Soldiers from Germany, called Hessians, fought for the British.

Visual Preview

Why did the war present challenges?

A Americans were eager to fight, but they lost many early battles.

B The British did not recognize the Americans' strengths or their own weaknesses.

C Americans had to support the Revolution on and off the battlefield.

D Americans faced serious economic problems during the Revolution.

Ⓐ READY FOR WAR?

By late August 1776, American soldiers under General Washington were eager to fight in the Revolution. But they were up against a powerful enemy—their home country, Great Britain.

The American soldiers and other Americans who supported the Revolution called themselves **Patriots**. Patriots are people who love their country. In the Revolution the Patriots were willing to fight to gain freedom from Great Britain. Yet few Patriot soldiers had ever fought on a battlefield. And they were about to fight the most powerful fighting force in the world—the British army.

Early Defeat

One of the earliest battles took place on Long Island, New York, on August 27, 1776. Here the 10,000-man American army faced 20,000 British soldiers.

The Patriots were badly beaten. In the following weeks, they lost several other battles around New York City. By October 1776 the British controlled New York City.

The British then chased Washington's army across the Hudson River. The Americans retreated across New Jersey. Many Patriots, including officers, began to question Washington's leadership.

QUICK CHECK

Main Idea and Details What happened to American soldiers in the early years of the Revolution?

Although they lacked training and supplies, Patriot soldiers often held off experienced British soldiers.

British soldiers

Patriot soldier

Patriot soldiers were eager to fight. But at first they were no match for the British army. Many British military leaders believed the war would end quickly. Instead, it lasted five years. The British had not counted on the Americans' strengths. And they did not recognize their own weaknesses.

BRITISH ARMY

Strengths

▶ **Army** The British had more than 60,000 soldiers in the American colonies. They included many **mercenaries**, professional soldiers from other countries. Most were Hessians from Germany.

▶ **Training** British soldiers were well-trained fighters who joined the army for life.

▶ **Equipment** Each soldier carried a gun called a musket tipped with a sharp bayonet.

▶ **Support** British soldiers were helped by **Loyalists**, colonists who supported Great Britain.

Weaknesses

▶ **Army** Soldiers and military supplies sent from Great Britain to the American colonies had to be shipped across the Atlantic Ocean.

▶ **Training** British soldiers trained to fight on open battlefields. But Patriots fired from hidden positions.

▶ **Equipment** The red uniform coats made British soldiers easy targets.

▶ **Support** Some British did not support the war because it raised the taxes they paid.

The British did not understand that the Patriots were willing to suffer a great deal to gain their freedom. Many Americans—those in the army and those at home—gave everything they had to win their independence.

QUICK CHECK

Main Idea and Details **What was the difference in training between Patriot soldiers and British soldiers?**

AMERICAN ARMY

Strengths

▶ **Army** Patriots fought to protect their homes, families, and a new nation.

▶ **Training** Patriots attacked by surprise, firing from well-protected spots. They used the tactics they learned during the French and Indian War.

▶ **Equipment** Many Patriot soldiers used Kentucky long rifles, which were more accurate than muskets.

▶ **Support** Citizens supported the army by making musket balls or blankets. Farmers gave food to soldiers.

Weaknesses

▶ **Army** General Washington never had more than 17,000 soldiers at any time in the war.

▶ **Training** Soldiers signed up for six months. That was not long enough to train to fight on open battlefields.

▶ **Equipment** Lack of uniforms, especially shoes, was a constant problem.

▶ **Support** Some Americans hid supplies or sold food to the army at high prices.

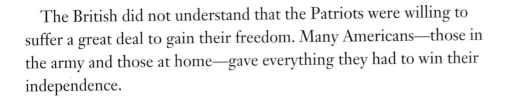

Americans supported the Revolution in many ways. Some raised money for the army or loaned money to the new government. Robert Morris, a wealthy merchant, loaned the new government $10,000—a huge amount then—to buy gunpowder, food, and supplies. Other Americans made weapons or ran businesses left behind by men who joined the army.

Support at Home

American women helped the fight for freedom in many ways. Some traveled to military camps. There they cooked meals or cared for sick and wounded soldiers.

Women also became carpenters, blacksmiths, and shipbuilders. Others took charge of family farms or shops when their husbands, fathers, or sons went to war.

Some women gave hope to Americans through writing. Mercy Otis Warren wrote a history of the American Revolution. Phillis Wheatley wrote poems about freedom.

Abigail Adams, the wife of John Adams, supported the Revolution from her home near Boston. You can read part of her letter about the Declaration of Independence below.

◄ Molly Pitcher loads a cannon.

Primary Sources

Last Thursday . . . I went . . . to Kings Street to hear the proclamation for independence read. . . . When Col(onel) Crafts read . . . great attention was given to every word. As soon as he ended . . . every face appeared joyful.

A section from a letter by Abigail Adams, July 21, 1776, Boston

Write About It It is 1776. Write a letter to a friend in another town describing the scene when the Declaration of Independence is read in your town square.

▲ This painting shows black soldiers from the First Rhode Island Regiment at the Battle of Newport.

Support in the Field

Several women helped on the battlefields. Sybil Luddington was called "the female Paul Revere" when she warned colonists of a British attack on Danbury, Connecticut. Deborah Sampson disguised herself as a man to join the army. Mary Ludwig Hays McCauley—we know her as "Molly Pitcher"—carried water to thirsty soldiers during battle. When her husband was wounded during the Battle of Monmouth, New Jersey, she took his place at the cannon.

African Americans were also encouraged to join the war. At this time, most African Americans in the colonies were enslaved and could not serve as soldiers at the beginning of the war. There were some free African American colonists who joined the American army. The words "all men are created equal" from the Declaration of Independence gave them hope that victory might create a new nation that treated all people equally.

About 5,000 African American colonists served with the Continental army. Rhode Island's African American soldiers formed their own unit in 1777, called the First Rhode Island Regiment. In 1781, the soldiers of the First Rhode Island Regiment fought in the final battle of the Revolution, a victory over the British at Yorktown, Virginia.

QUICK CHECK

Main Idea and Details How did the Revolution change the roles of colonial women?

175

D WARTIME SHORTAGES

Paper Dollars Equaling One-Dollar Coin, 1777–1781

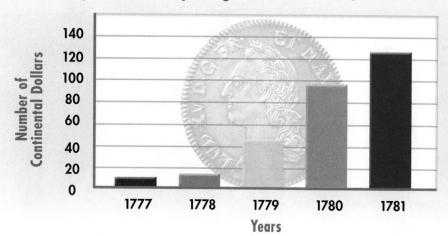

Number of Continental Dollars — Years: 1777, 1778, 1779, 1780, 1781

Chart Skill

In 1779 about how many Continental dollars would you need to buy an item worth a one-dollar coin?

Patriot soldiers faced many shortages during the war. However, most Americans also lacked food and clothing. Items such as cloth, kettles, and tools were made in British factories—and all trade was cut off when the fighting began.

Unfair Practices

Americans themselves caused other shortages. Hoarding, or hiding away goods, such as flour, molasses, and manufactured items was a serious problem. Hoarding made these products hard to get—which raised their price. Some farmers and merchants became wealthy by **profiteering**, or charging high prices, for goods they hoarded.

Printing Money

Profiteering also hurt the government. Forced to pay high prices for supplies, Congress printed more paper money called "Continentals." However, the treasury did not have enough gold to back up their value. The drop in the value of Continentals led to **inflation**. Inflation is a large and rapid rise in prices. People at the time described something that was useless as "not worth a Continental."

QUICK CHECK

Main Idea and Details **How did profiteering hurt Americans?**

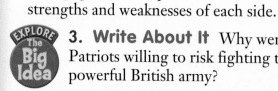

Check Understanding

1. **VOCABULARY** Use two words below in a sentence about economic problems.

   Patriot   profiteering
   mercenary   inflation
   Loyalist

2. **READING SKILL** Main Idea and Details Use the chart from page 170 to explain the strengths and weaknesses of each side.

Main Idea	Details

   EXPLORE The Big Idea 3. **Write About It** Why were Patriots willing to risk fighting the powerful British army?

Map and Globe Skills

Use a Battle Map

VOCABULARY

battle map

One way to study historical battles is to look at a **battle map**. A battle map shows important places, actions, and troop movements during a battle. The map on this page explains an early battle of the American Revolution, the Battle of Bunker Hill, which took place in June 1775.

Learn It

● Look at the map key, or legend. It tells the meaning of the symbols on the map. On this map, the red-coated figures show British troops. The blue-coated figures show American troops. Arrows show the directions troops moved. Bursts show where the actual fighting took place.

● Look for a scale to find out how far troops traveled. Look at the compass to tell you in which direction they moved.

Try It

● What direction is Bunker Hill from Breed's Hill?

● On what hill did most of the fighting take place?

● How far did British troops have to travel by water and land to fight the Americans?

Apply It

● What information can you get from a battle map that is not in the text?

● Write one sentence that tells what you have learned about the Battle of Bunker Hill from the map.

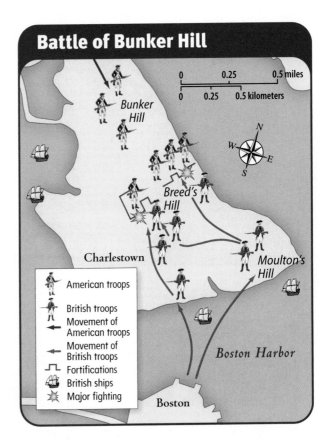

Battle of Bunker Hill

Bunker Hill

Breed's Hill

Charlestown

Moulton's Hill

Boston Harbor

Boston

0   0.25   0.5 miles
0   0.25   0.5 kilometers

American troops
British troops
Movement of American troops
Movement of British troops
Fortifications
British ships
Major fighting

AMERICAN VICTORIES

Lesson 7

VOCABULARY

desert p. 179

Treaty of Alliance p. 181

READING SKILL

Main Idea and Details

Copy the chart below. Fill in the main idea and details of events that happened between 1776 and 1778.

Main Idea	Details

Illinois Learning Standards

16.A.2b, 16.B.2b (US)

Washington won victories in New Jersey in 1776 and early 1777.

Visual Preview

How did Patriots influence the war?

A In 1776 the Patriots won an important battle at Trenton, New Jersey.

B The Patriot victory at Saratoga, New York, in 1777 was a turning point.

C Americans faced a hard winter and won victories outside the colonies and at sea.

178

Ⓐ MAJOR PATRIOT VICTORY

*The final weeks of 1776 were dark days for the Patriots.
General Washington's army had lost battles around New York City.
Now British troops chased the Patriots
across New Jersey into Pennsylvania.*

Writer Thomas Paine was among the Patriot soldiers escaping to Pennsylvania. In a pamphlet titled *The Crisis*, he described those dark days with these words:

> These are the times that try men's souls.

Washington led the Patriots across the icy Delaware River. ▲

Victory in New Jersey

By December 25, many Patriot soldiers had left the army. Some chose to **desert**, or run away. Many who remained had no shoes or supplies. Without a victory to give Americans hope, Washington believed the Revolution would fail. So, he came up with a bold new plan.

Washington decided to cross the Delaware River from Pennsylvania and attack the Hessian soldiers in Trenton, New Jersey, on Christmas night. An icy storm blew in on December 25 and the Patriots finally reached New Jersey at

4 A.M. Washington's plan worked. At Trenton, the surprised Hessians quickly surrendered. Washington lost only two men in the battle—both froze to death.

On January 3, 1777, the Patriots defeated the British at Princeton, New Jersey, and captured badly needed supplies from the British. Now Patriot soldiers had food, weapons, shoes—and hope.

QUICK CHECK

Main Idea and Details Why did George Washington come up with a bold plan?

BATTLE OF SARATOGA

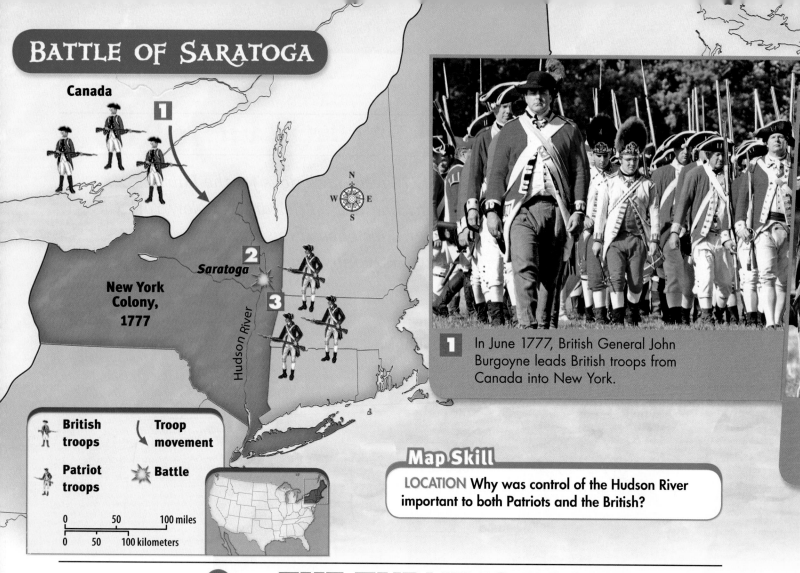

Canada

1

New York Colony, 1777

Saratoga **2**

3

Hudson River

1 In June 1777, British General John Burgoyne leads British troops from Canada into New York.

British troops

Troop movement

Patriot troops

Battle

| 0 | 50 | 100 miles |
| 0 | 50 | 100 kilometers |

Map Skill

LOCATION Why was control of the Hudson River important to both Patriots and the British?

B THE TURNING POINT

A turning point is an event that causes an important change. For the Patriots, the Battle of Saratoga became a turning point in the Revolutionary War.

Victory at Saratoga

In June 1777, British General John Burgoyne led several thousand soldiers from Canada into New York. He believed another British force would march north. A Patriot force under General Horatio Gates would then be trapped between them.

At first, Burgoyne's army drove Gates and the Patriots south. But the British supply wagons got stuck on forest roads. The Patriots

had time to gather more troops and decided to stand and fight at Saratoga, New York. Burgoyne reached Saratoga on September 16. By then, Gates had three times more soldiers than the British general. The Patriots had also built dirt walls at Bemis Heights, near Saratoga.

On September 19, British and Patriot troops battled at Freeman's Farm, near Saratoga. The British won control of the farm. But they lost more soldiers than the Patriots. Low on troops, Burgoyne needed help—but no army marched north. Finally, he could wait no longer. On October 7, British soldiers battled Patriot soldiers at Bemis Heights. The British

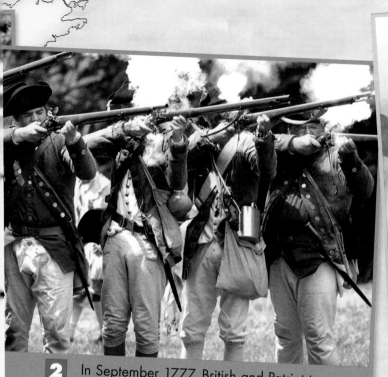

2 In September 1777, British and Patriot troops battle at Freeman's Farm outside Saratoga. The British take control of the farm but suffer heavy losses.

3 In October 1777, British General Burgoyne orders an attack on Bemis Heights near Saratoga and is defeated.

had no chance to win. Burgoyne surrendered on October 17, 1777. The British defeat at Saratoga changed the outcome of the war.

Help from Europe

When news of the Patriot victory reached Paris, France, it convinced the French that the Americans could win independence from Great Britain. As a result, the French and American governments signed a **Treaty of Alliance**, or an agreement to work together. Several months later, French troops, warships, and supplies began the journey across the Atlantic Ocean.

Other Europeans who supported the Patriots also came to America to join the fight. Thaddeus Kosciuszko, an engineer educated in Poland, arrived to help build forts. One young French citizen who arrived to help the Patriots

was 19-year-old Marquis de Lafayette. When Lafayette met George Washington, the two became close friends.

QUICK CHECK

Main Idea and Details Why did France agree to help the United States fight Great Britain?

PEOPLE

The dirt walls at Bemis Heights in Saratoga were designed by **Thaddeus Kosciuszko**, an engineer educated in Poland. He came to America to join the Patriots and later designed the fort at West Point, New York.

Thaddeus Kosciuszko

VALLEY FORGE AND BEYOND

The victory at Saratoga did not help the Patriots right away. In the winter of 1777 to 1778, Washington's troops faced bitter cold as they huddled around campfires at Valley Forge, Pennsylvania.

Hunger and Disease

For the first two months of that winter, soldiers lived in ragged tents. Few had shoes or blankets, and they shared coats and gloves. Food was in short supply too. At Valley Forge the main food was "fire cakes," a paste of flour and water roasted on a stick over campfires. Weak from cold and hunger, soldiers became sick. Diseases spread quickly because soldiers lived close together. At least 2,500 died from illnesses such as typhoid, influenza, and smallpox.

During that cold winter, a military instructor named Baron Friedrich von Steuben arrived from the German kingdom of Prussia. He saw that the American army needed strict training. Von Steuben taught the Patriots to march in rows and fight together instead of separately. By June 1778, the American army had become a well-trained fighting force able to defeat the British on open battlefields.

Fighting Outside the Colonies

Not all important Revolutionary battles were fought in the 13 Colonies. Key battles took place in the British territories west of the Appalachian Mountains—and even off the coast of Great Britain.

General Washington and his tired soldiers march into Valley Forge. Many soldiers deserted because of the terrible conditions.

George Washington

In February 1779, George Rogers Clark and his men marched for days across swampland. After marching for a month, the Americans attacked and defeated the British at Fort Sackville near present-day Vincennes, Indiana.

The greatest hero of the American navy was John Paul Jones. On September 23, 1779, his ship, the *Bonhomme Richard*, defeated the British warship *Serapis* off the coast of Great Britain. Today, John Paul Jones is known as the "Father of the American Navy."

QUICK CHECK

Main Idea and Details How did training at Valley Forge help the Patriot army?

Check Understanding

1. **VOCABULARY** Use each vocabulary term below in a sentence.

   desert   **Treaty of Alliance**

2. **READING SKILL** Main Idea and Details Use the chart from page 178 to write about the winter at Valley Forge.

Main Idea	Details

3. **Write About It** Why did Burgoyne risk an attack on Bemis Heights?

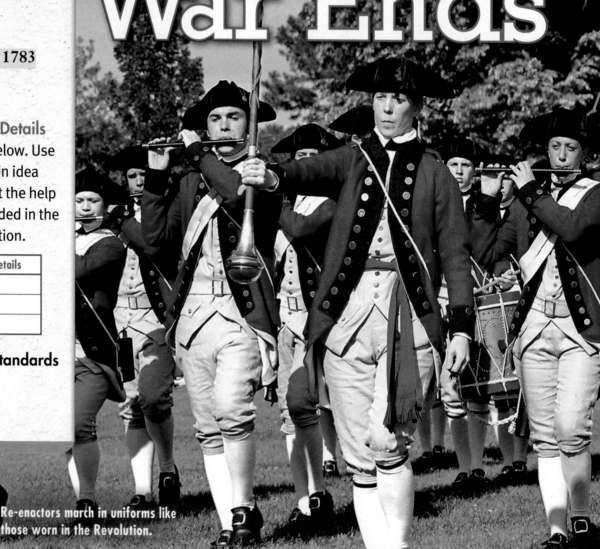

The War Ends

Lesson 8

VOCABULARY

blockade p. 187

Treaty of Paris 1783 p. 187

READING SKILL

Main Idea and Details

Copy the chart below. Use it to fill in the main idea and details about the help that France provided in the Amercian Revolution.

Main Idea	Details

Illinois Learning Standards
16.B.2b (US)

Re-enactors march in uniforms like those worn in the Revolution.

Visual Preview

How did the Revolution affect life in America?

A Spain helped the Patriots as the war moved to the South.

B The British surrendered at Yorktown, Virginia, in 1781.

C Loyalists, Native Americans, and enslaved Africans faced new challenges.

A THE WAR MOVES SOUTH

By 1779 the British hoped to win the war in a region with a large Loyalist population—the Southern colonies. Controlling the wealthy Southern colonies became the main goal of British leaders.

The British plan to keep control of the South did not begin well. In 1779 the Americans gained support from Spain, a French ally. The Spanish government loaned money to the Patriots. In addition, Bernardo de Gálvez, the governor of Spain's Louisiana Territory, closed the port at New Orleans to Great Britain and opened it to American ships.

Meanwhile, George Washington appointed General Nathanael Greene to lead Patriot forces in the South. However, the Patriots continued to face problems. Congress had little money to pay troops, and supplies were low. Between 1778 and 1781, the British army won battles at Savannah, Georgia, and at Charles Town and Camden in South Carolina.

Costly Victory

For a time, it seemed that the British would remain in control of the South. But their victories were costly. In 1780 General Charles Cornwallis took command of the British army in the South. Cornwallis pursued the American army north through the Carolinas. The two armies finally met in March 1781 at Guilford Court House, North Carolina.

British General Lord Cornwallis

The British won the battle, but Cornwallis lost one-fourth of his soldiers. However, he claimed a British victory because Greene's forces left the battlefield. When one British leader learned of the many troops lost, he said:

"Another such victory would destroy the British army."

QUICK CHECK

Main Idea and Details What took place between 1779 and 1781 in the Revolution?

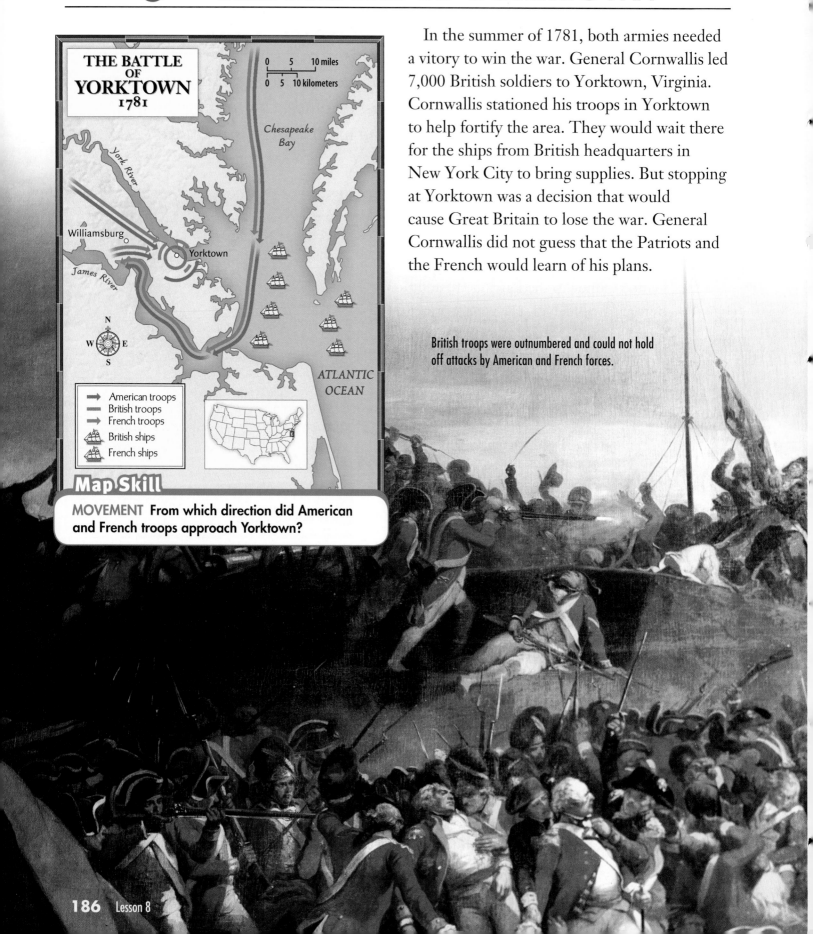

THE BATTLE OF YORKTOWN

THE BATTLE OF YORKTOWN 1781

0   5   10 miles
0   5   10 kilometers

Chesapeake Bay

York River

Williamsburg

Yorktown

James River

N
W   E
S

ATLANTIC OCEAN

→ American troops
→ British troops
→ French troops
⛵ British ships
⛵ French ships

Map Skill

MOVEMENT From which direction did American and French troops approach Yorktown?

In the summer of 1781, both armies needed a vitory to win the war. General Cornwallis led 7,000 British soldiers to Yorktown, Virginia. Cornwallis stationed his troops in Yorktown to help fortify the area. They would wait there for the ships from British headquarters in New York City to bring supplies. But stopping at Yorktown was a decision that would cause Great Britain to lose the war. General Cornwallis did not guess that the Patriots and the French would learn of his plans.

British troops were outnumbered and could not hold off attacks by American and French forces.

Lafayette's Plan

Not far from Yorktown, Marquis de Lafayette commanded a small Patriot army. His troops were no match for Cornwallis. However, Lafayette had one advantage. One of Cornwallis's servants, James Armistead, was a spy for Lafayette. Armistead passed on information that the British were waiting for supplies from New York. Lafayette sent this information to the French navy. French warships off the Atlantic coast set up a **blockade** of British ships. A blockade is an action that prevents the passage of people or supplies. The French ships kept British troops and supplies from reaching Cornwallis.

Marquis de Lafayette

At the same time, Washington's army and a large French force joined Lafayette. Cornwallis discovered too late that his army was surrounded by a French and Patriot army of more than 16,000 men.

French and American troops battled the British army for weeks, pounding the British with continuous cannon fire. Some American cannons became so hot from constant firing that they began to melt. To escape the cannon fire, Cornwallis ordered 2,000 men into boats to flee across the York River. But a fierce storm blew in, stopping the escape. On October 17, 1781, Cornwallis sent a runner to surrender to Washington.

The Revolution Ends

Soon after the surrender, the British government began peace talks with France, Spain, and the Americans in Paris, France. **The Treaty of Paris 1783** ended the American Revolution. Under the agreement Great Britain recognized American independence. The Mississippi River became the new nation's western border. The treaty also opened the Mississippi River to ships from France, Spain, Britain, and the United States.

The American Revolution was over. The 13 colonies were now known as the United States. In his farewell orders to the Continental army, Washington wrote that the determination of the troops:

> **"**through almost every possible suffering and discouragement for the space of eight long years, was little short of a standing miracle.**"**

QUICK CHECK

Main Idea and Details **How did Cornwallis's decision to stop at Yorktown lead to Great Britain's defeat?**

187

ⓒ THE RESULTS OF THE WAR

Several years after the Revolution, John Adams was asked about the war. He said that there had been two revolutions. One was the war itself. The other was:

> **❝in the minds and hearts of the people.❞**

The United States had won independence. But not all the hearts and minds of the people had been changed.

Loyalists Leave

When the war ended, about 60,000 Loyalists remained in the United States. Many of these people had been wealthy merchants before the war. Some had been forced to give up their homes and property during the fighting. After the war, many Loyalists moved to Canada, which remained a British colony. Other Loyalists remained in the United States and tried to fit in with the new society. Many former Loyalists decided to move to the Western frontier.

Native Americans Lose Lands

During the Revolutionary War most Native Americans, including Joseph Brant who led several Native American groups, sided with the British. This was because Great Britain had protected Native American lands west of the Appalachians from American settlement.

◀ This illustration of Patriot soldiers returning from the American Revolution appeared in a magazine for young people in 1906.

Native Americans had fought to protect their own homelands, but many Americans saw them as enemies. As a result, settlers felt no guilt about taking land from people who had fought with the British.

Slavery Continues

In the Declaration of Independence, the phrase "all men are created equal" led some people to believe that slavery might end. The new American government, however, needed the support of Southern plantation owners who depended on the labor of enslaved Africans. As a result, slavery continued in the new nation.

QUICK CHECK

Main Idea and Details **What were the results of the American Revolution?**

Check Understanding

1. **VOCABULARY** Write one sentence using both terms below.

   blockade   **Treaty of Paris 1783**

2. **READING SKILL** Main Idea and Details Use the chart from page 184 to write a paragraph about France's role at the Battle of Yorktown.

Main Idea	Details

3. **Write About It** Make a list of the reasons people in the following groups risked their lives in the war: Patriots, Loyalists, British soldiers, African Americans, and Native Americans.

Unit 4 Review and Assess

Vocabulary

Number a paper from 1 to 4. Match each description below with the correct term.

mercenary   **Treaty of Paris 1783**

patriot   **boycott**

1. Someone who loves his or her country

2. The agreement that ended the American Revolution

3. To refuse to buy goods or services from a person, group or country.

4. Someone who is paid to fight for another country

Comprehension and Critical Thinking

5. How did women in the colonies help fight for independence during the Revolutionary War?

6. **Reading Skill** How did colonists protest against British laws and regulations?

7. **Critical Thinking** How did African Americans feel that the struggle for independence would help them?

8. **Critical Thinking** How did the victory at Yorktown affect Loyalists and Native Americans?

Skill

Use a Battle Map

Look at map on the right. Write a complete sentence to answer each question.

9. What body of water was the scene of major fighting?

10. Based on the map, what do you think was one major difference in the fortifications of the British and the Americans?

Battle of Saratoga

Major fighting
Headquarters
Building
Fortification
British troops
American troops

Freeman's Farm
Burgoyne's Headquarters
To Saratoga
Mill Creek
BEMIS HEIGHTS
Hudson River
Gates's Headquarters
To Albany

0   0.25   0.5 miles
0   0.25 0.5 kilometers

Illinois Standards Achievement Test Preparation

Thomas Jefferson worked on writing the Declaration of Independence for two weeks. When he was satisfied, he read it to Benjamin Franklin and John Adams. They made a few changes and then presented it to the Continental Congress on June 28.

On July 1, 1776, the Continental Congress began discussing the Declaration of Independence. Three days later, it was approved. Church bells rang across Philadelphia to tell people the good news. The Declaration was then copied on paper made of sheepskin. On August 2, John Hancock was first to sign—in large letters. Today a person's signature is sometimes called a "John Hancock".

1

The main idea of this passage is about—

Ⓐ Thomas Jefferson's life.
Ⓑ the friendship between Thomas Jefferson and Benjamin Franklin.
Ⓒ the creation of the Declaration of Independence.
Ⓓ the powers of Congress.

2

According to the passage, how long did it take Congress to approve the Declaration of Independence?

Ⓐ Two weeks
Ⓑ Three days
Ⓒ Six days
Ⓓ One month

3

A person would most likely read this passage to—

Ⓐ learn about Philadelphia.
Ⓑ discover new uses for sheep skin.
Ⓒ learn about the Declaration of Independence.
Ⓓ understand the duties of Congress.

4

Why do some people refer to a signature as a "John Hancock"?

Ⓐ He wrote the Declaration of Independence.
Ⓑ He was the first to sign the Declaration of Independence.
Ⓒ He created the ballpoint pen.
Ⓓ He created the printing press.

Why do people take risks?

Write About the Big Idea

Expository Essay
Use the Unit 4 foldable to help you write an essay that answers the Big Idea question, *Why do people take risks?* Be sure to begin your essay with an introduction. Use the notes you wrote under each tab in the foldable for details to support each main idea. End with a concluding paragraph that answers the question.

Risks

French   British   American

Make a Leadership Yearbook

Work in small groups to make a yearbook of leaders that you have read about in Unit 4. Each group should choose a different leader. Here's how to make your yearbook page.

1. Have one person find or draw a picture of the leader's face or a picture of that person in action.

2. Have one person write down the years the leader lived and important events in his or her life. Use a quote if possible.

3. Work as a group to list at least three leadership qualities of the person you have chosen.

When each group has finished its page, join all of the pages together to make a book. Decide as a class what picture or words should appear on the cover.

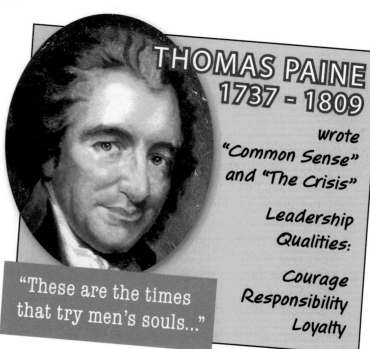

THOMAS PAINE
1737 – 1809

wrote "Common Sense" and "The Crisis"

Leadership Qualities:

Courage
Responsibility
Loyalty

"These are the times that try men's souls..."

Reference Section

The Reference Section is a collection of tools that can be used to help you understand the information you read in this textbook.

Unit 1 • Reading Skills

Compare and Contrast

When you compare, you notice how things are alike. When you contrast, you notice how they are different. Comparing and contrasting will help you understand the people and events you read about in social studies.

Learn It

- To compare two things, note how they are similar. The words *alike*, *same*, and *both* are clues to similarities.

- To contrast two things, note how they are different. The words *different, however,* and *by contrast* show differences.

- Now read the passage below. Think about how you would compare and contrast Native American groups.

Native Peoples of North America

Contrast
The first paragraph is a contrast between environments.

For Native Americans in the West, environment helped to determine culture. The Arctic is extremely cold. By contrast, the hot, dry deserts of southern California are very hot. Each culture adapted to the climate and natural resources of their surroundings.

The Inuit in Alaska found ways to live in the bitterly cold Arctic. On hunting trips, men built igloos, temporary shelters, of snow blocks. In warm weather, hunters made tents from wooden poles and animal skins. The Inuit hunted walruses, seals, fish, and whales.

Contrast
This sentence tells how groups were different.

Life in the desert of southern California was very different from life in the Arctic. Desert groups such as the Cahuilla used desert plants for food. They also grew crops using irrigation. The Cahuilla dug wells in the desert sand. They watered fields of maize, squash, and beans. Like the Inuit, desert groups hunted animals.

Compare
This shows how groups were alike.

Try It

Copy the Venn diagram. Then fill in the left-hand side with Inuit activities. Fill in the right-hand side with desert group activities. Fill in the center with activities that both groups did.

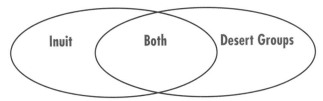

How did you figure out the similarities and differences?

Apply It

- Review the steps for comparing and contrasting in Learn It.

- Read the passage below. Use a Venn diagram to show the similarities and differences between the Creek and the Iroquois.

One Southern woodlands group, the Creek, arranged their towns around a large council house or "Chokofa." Family homes called wattle-and-daub huts were made from poles and covered with grass, mud, or thatch. Unlike the Creek, the Iroquois of the northern woodlands lived in longhouses. Longhouses were large enough for several families and were made of bent poles covered with sheets of bark. The longest longhouse is thought to have been about 340 feet. That's longer than a football field!

Both the Creek and Iroquois celebrated the Green Corn Festival, honoring the summer's first maize crop. They also played a sport with sticks that French explorers later called Lacrosse. Lacrosse games were sometimes played to settle disagreements.

Unit 2 • Reading Skills

Cause and Effect

A cause is an action or event that makes something else happen. An effect is the result of the cause. When one event causes another event to happen, the two events have a cause-and-effect relationship. Connecting causes with effects will help you understand more about what you read in social studies.

Learn It

- After you finish reading a section, ask yourself, "What happened?" The answer to that question will help you identify an effect.

- Then ask yourself "Why did that happen?" The answer to this question helps you identify a cause.

- Look for the clue words *because, so,* and *as a result.* These words point to cause-and-effect relationships.

- Now read the passage below. Use the steps above to pick out cause-and-effect relationships.

Exploration and Colonization

The first people of the Middle Ages to travel to distant regions were the Norse, or "north people," who lived in what are today Denmark, Sweden, and Norway. To gain wealth, they sailed throughout Europe by ocean and rivers trading goods. Some people knew them as Vikings, a Norse word for "raiders."

Around A.D. 1000, Viking explorers were the first to reach North America. But their settlements there did not last. As a result, the Vikings' discoveries were forgotten for many years.

Cause
This is a cause. It tells why.

Effect
This is an effect. It tells what happened.

Cause and Effect
This has a cause and an effect.

Try It

Copy and complete the cause and effect chart below. Then fill in the chart with another cause and effect from the paragraph.

Cause	→	Effect
	→	
	→	
	→	

How did you figure out the causes and effects?

Apply It

- Review the steps for understanding cause and effect in Learn It.

- Read the passage below. Then use a chart to list the causes and effects from the passage.

In 1096 thousands of Europeans began the long journey southeast to Jerusalem. The city had great religious importance to Jews, Christians, and Muslims. European Christians hoped to capture the city from the Muslim Turks who ruled the city at the time. These journeys were called Crusades. The Crusaders captured Jerusalem, but were driven out after about 100 years.

Many European travelers returned with products of these cultures, such as cloth or spices, that were unknown in Europe. Traders found that Europeans were willing to pay a lot for items such as cotton, pepper, and cinnamon.

Make Generalizations

When you read, sometimes it helps to make a generalization. A generalization is a broad statement that shows how different facts, people, or events have something in common. Being able to make generalizations will help you uncover similarities that you might otherwise not notice. Generalizations can also help you make sense of new information you will learn later.

Learn It

- Identify text clues with similarities or relationships.

- Apply what you already know about the topic.

- Make a generalization that is true about all of your text clues and what you know.

- Read the passage below. Think about a generalization you could make.

Text Clue Puritans wanted self-government.	
Text Clue Elections were held at town meetings.	
Text Clue Only white men who were Puritans voted.	

Colonial America

The Puritans' charter allowed them to govern themselves. They held elections at town hall meetings, but only white men who were Puritans could vote. John Winthrop was elected the first governor of the Puritans. Winthrop wrote about building "a city upon a hill" that would show how God wanted people to live.

Try It

Copy and complete the generalization chart below. Then make a generalization about the Puritan government.

Text Clues	What You Know	Generalization

How did you figure out how to make a generalization?

Apply It

● Review the steps to make generalizations in Learn It.

● Read the next paragraph. Then make a generalization about Roger Williams using a generalizations chart.

One person who disagreed with Puritan leaders was Roger Williams. He believed that government should tolerate people with different religious views. To tolerate means to allow people to have beliefs or behaviors that are different from others. Puritans accused Williams of spreading "new and dangerous opinions" and tried to silence him. Williams decided to move south where he lived with the Narragansett Indians. In 1636 Williams bought land from the Narragansett and founded the settlement of Providence in what became Rhode Island. It was the first colony to allow freedom of religion.

Main Idea and Details

As you read, it is important to look for the main idea and supporting details. The main idea is what a paragraph is all about. The details tell about, or support, the main idea. Often the main idea is stated in the first sentence of a paragraph. At other times, you have to figure out the main idea. Either way, keeping track of the main idea and details will help you understand what you read.

Learn It

● Think about what a paragraph is all about. Look to see if the first sentence states the main idea.

● Look for details. Think about the idea that the details tell about.

● Now read the paragraph below. Look for the main idea and details.

Main Idea:
This sentence states the main idea.

Supporting Detail
This detail explains that some colonists worked for the British government.

Supporting Detail
This detail also supports the main idea.

The American Revolution

While most colonists wanted to end what they saw as British bullying, not all colonists wanted to end their ties to Great Britain. They hoped that the British government would compromise to end the fighting. Some of these colonists worked for the British government. Others feared that they might lose their property during the fighting. Still others simply did not want to separate from Great Britain; they hoped for compromise.

Try It

Copy and complete the chart below. Then fill in the chart by listing the main idea and details from the paragraph on page R8.

Main Idea	Details

How did you choose the main idea and details?

Apply It

- Read the paragraph below. Then create supporting details using the information.

- Review the steps for finding the main idea and details. Then read the paragraph below. Create a main idea and supporting details chart using the information.

   Most colonists understood that a compromise would not be reached. They knew that once British soldiers were killed, the British government would not back down. The events around Boston made colonists see themselves in a new way. They were no longer British citizens living in colonies. They were citizens of a new country that was fighting to free itself from British rule. They were Americans.

Geography Handbook

Geography and You

Many people think geography means learning about the location of cities, states, and countries, but geography is much more than that. Geography is the study of our Earth and all its people. Geography includes learning about bodies of water such as oceans, lakes, and rivers. Geography helps us learn about landforms such as plains and mountains. Geography also helps us learn about using land and water wisely.

People are an important part of the study of geography. Geography includes the study of how people adapt to live in new places. How people move, how they transport goods, and how ideas travel from place to place are also parts of geography.

In fact, geography has so many parts that geographers have divided the information into smaller groups to help people understand its ideas. These groups are called the six elements of geography.

Six Elements of Geography

The World in Spatial Terms: Where is a place located, and what land or water features does that place have?

Places and Regions: What is special about a place, and what makes it different from other places?

Physical Systems: What has shaped the land and climate of a place, and how does this affect the plants, animals, and people there?

Human Systems: How do people, ideas, and goods move from place to place?

Environment and Society: How have people changed the land and water of a place, and how have land and water affected the people who live in a place?

Uses of Geography: How has geography influenced events in the past, and how will it influence events now and in the future?

Five Themes of Geography

You have read about the six elements of geography. The five themes of geography are another way of dividing the ideas of geography. The themes, or topics, are **location**, **place**, **region**, **movement**, and **human interaction**. Using these five themes is another way to understand events you read about in this book.

1. Location

The White House

In geography, *location* means an exact spot on the planet. A location is usually a street name and number. You write a location when you address a letter.

2. Place

The Grand Canyon

A *place* is described by its physical features, such as rivers, mountains, or valleys. Human features, such as cities, language, and traditions can also describe a place.

3. Region

Wheat field in the Midwest

A *region* is larger than a place or location. The people in a region are affected by landforms. Their region has typical jobs and customs. For example, the fertile soil of the Mississippi lowlands helps farmers in the region grow crops.

4. Movement

Passenger train

Throughout history, people have moved to find better land or a better life. Geographers study why these *movements* occurred. They also study how people's movements have changed a region.

5. Human Interaction

Hoover Dam

Geographers study the ways that people adapt to their environment. Geographers also study how people change their environment. The *interaction* between people and their environment explains how land is used.

Dictionary of Geographic Terms

1 **BASIN** A bowl-shaped landform surrounded by higher land

2 **BAY** Part of an ocean or lake that extends deeply into the land

3 **CANAL** A channel built to carry water for irrigation or transportation

4 **CANYON** A deep, narrow valley with steep sides

5 **COAST** The land along an ocean

6 **DAM** A wall built across a river, creating a lake that stores water

7 **DELTA** Land made of soil left behind as a river drains into a larger body of water

8 **DESERT** A dry environment with few plants and animals

9 **FAULT** The border between two of the plates that make up Earth's crust

10 **GLACIER** A huge sheet of ice that moves slowly across the land

11 **GULF** Part of an ocean that extends into the land; larger than a bay

12 **HARBOR** A sheltered place along a coast where boats dock safely

13 **HILL** A rounded, raised landform; not as high as a mountain

14 **ISLAND** A body of land completely surrounded by water

15 **LAKE** A body of water completely surrounded by land

16 **MESA** A hill with a flat top; smaller than a plateau

17 **MOUNTAIN** A high landform with steep sides; higher than a hill

18 **MOUNTAIN PASS** A narrow gap through a mountain range

19 **MOUTH** The place where a river empties into a larger body of water

20 **OCEAN** A large body of salt water; oceans cover much of Earth's surface

21 **PENINSULA** A body of land nearly surrounded by water

22 **PLAIN** A large area of nearly flat land

23 **PLATEAU** A high, flat area that rises steeply above the surrounding land

24 **PORT** A place where ships load and unload their goods

25 **RESERVOIR** A natural or artificial lake used to store water

26 **RIVER** A large stream that empties into another body of water

27 **SOURCE** The starting point of a river

28 **VALLEY** An area of low land between hills or mountains

29 **VOLCANO** An opening in Earth's surface through which hot rock and ash are forced out

30 **WATERFALL** A flow of water falling vertically

Read a Map

Maps are drawings of places on Earth. Most maps have standard features to help you read the map. Some important information you get from a map is direction. The main directions are north, south, east, and west. These are called cardinal directions.

The areas between the cardinal directions are called intermediate directions. These are northeast, southeast, southwest, and northwest. You use these directions to describe one place in relation to another.

In what direction is Iowa from North Carolina?

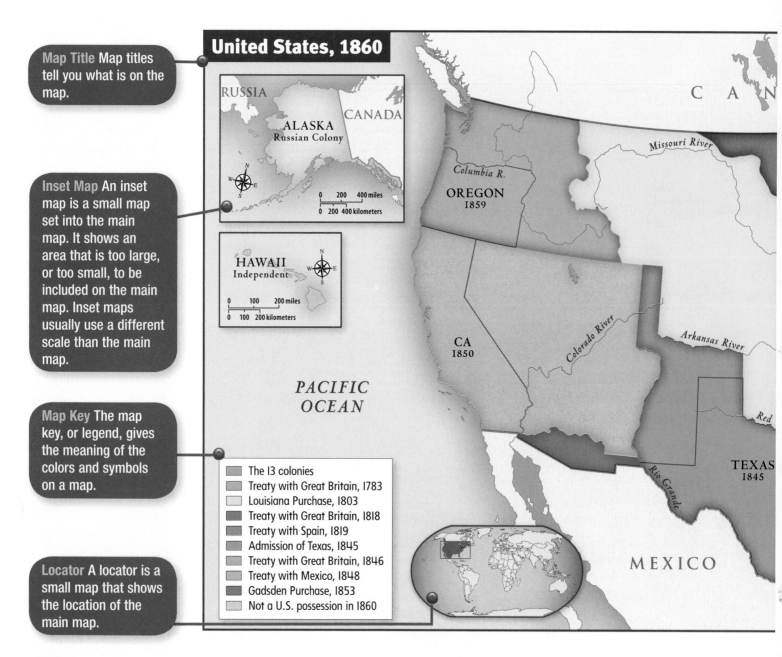

Map Title Map titles tell you what is on the map.

Inset Map An inset map is a small map set into the main map. It shows an area that is too large, or too small, to be included on the main map. Inset maps usually use a different scale than the main map.

Map Key The map key, or legend, gives the meaning of the colors and symbols on a map.

Locator A locator is a small map that shows the location of the main map.

United States, 1860

RUSSIA

ALASKA
Russian Colony

CANADA

0   200   400 miles
0   200 400 kilometers

HAWAII
Independent

0   100   200 miles
0   100   200 kilometers

CANADA

Missouri River

Columbia R.

OREGON
1859

CA
1850

Colorado River

Arkansas River

PACIFIC
OCEAN

Red

TEXAS
1845

Rio Grande

MEXICO

The 13 colonies
Treaty with Great Britain, 1783
Louisiana Purchase, 1803
Treaty with Great Britain, 1818
Treaty with Spain, 1819
Admission of Texas, 1845
Treaty with Great Britain, 1846
Treaty with Mexico, 1848
Gadsden Purchase, 1853
Not a U.S. possession in 1860

Read Historical Maps

Some maps capture a period in time. These are called historical maps. They show information about past events or places. For example, this map shows the United States in 1860 just before the beginning of the Civil War. Read the title and the key to understand the information on the map.

What year did California become a state?

Which states entered the Union after California?

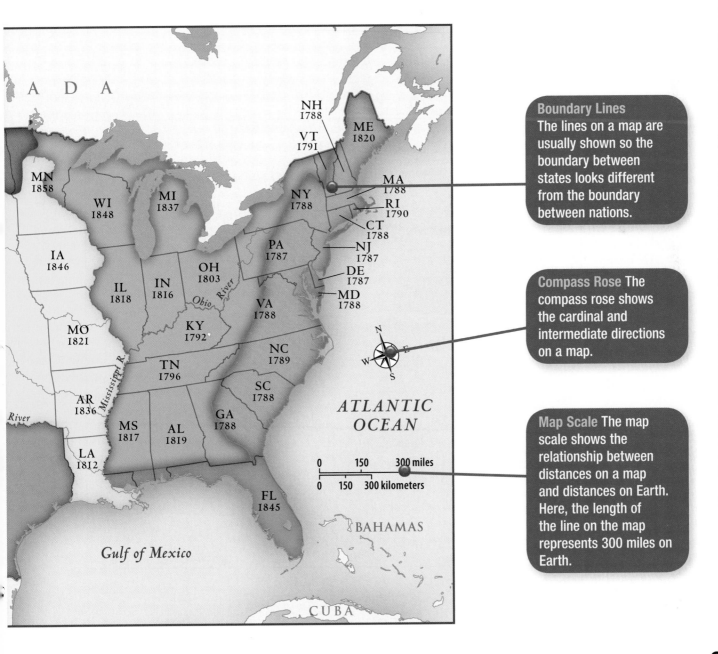

Boundary Lines
The lines on a map are usually shown so the boundary between states looks different from the boundary between nations.

Compass Rose The compass rose shows the cardinal and intermediate directions on a map.

Map Scale The map scale shows the relationship between distances on a map and distances on Earth. Here, the length of the line on the map represents 300 miles on Earth.

Use Elevation Maps

An elevation map is a physical map that uses colors to show the elevation, or height of land above or below sea level. The height is usually measured in feet or meters. Sea level is measured as 0 feet or meters around the world. Read the key to understand what each color means. The map on this page uses purple to show land below sea level.

Identify the area of your town or city on the map. How high above sea level is your area?

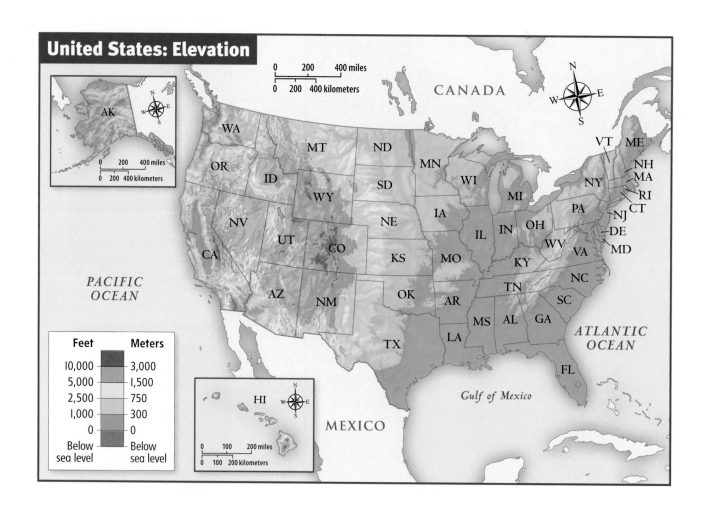

Use Road Maps

Suppose you want to go somewhere you have never been before. How do you know what road to take? You could use a road map. Road maps show where the roads in a certain area go. By reading a road map you can figure out how to get from one place to another.

Look at the road map of Indiana. The map key tells you which kinds of roads are shown on the map. Interstate highways run through two or more states and have two or more lanes in each direction. U.S. highways are usually two lane highways that also connect states. State highways stop at a state's borders. The name of each highway is a number. Notice the different symbols for each of the three kinds of highways.

Which roads would you use to get from South Bend to Terre Haute?

Hemispheres

The equator is an imaginary line on Earth. It divides the sphere of Earth in half. A word for half a sphere is *hemisphere*. The prefix "hemi" means half. Geographers divide Earth into four hemispheres.

All land and ocean north of the equator is in the Northern Hemisphere. All the land and ocean south of the equator is in the Southern Hemisphere.

Another imaginary line on Earth runs from the North Pole to the South Pole. It is called the prime meridian. It divides Earth into the Eastern Hemisphere and the Western Hemisphere.

Is North America in the Northern Hemisphere or Southern Hemisphere?

Is North America in the Eastern Hemisphere or the Western Hemisphere?

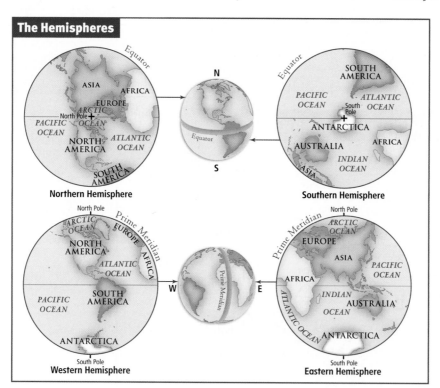

The Hemispheres

Earth-Sun Relationships

Earth revolves around the sun once a year. As it revolves, Earth also rotates on an axis. An axis is an imaginary line through the center of an object. Earth's axis is tilted 23.5° from due north. That tilt, plus the revolution of Earth around the sun, causes the seasons. The seasons are opposite in the Southern and Northern Hemispheres. For example, when it is winter in the Northern Hemisphere, it is summer in the Southern Hemisphere.

Latitude and Longitude

Geographers have created an imaginary system of lines on the Earth. These lines form a grid to help locate places on any part of the globe. Lines of latitude go from east to west. Lines of longitude go from north to south.

Lines of latitude are called parallels because they are an equal distance apart. The lines of latitude are numbered from 0 at the equator to 90 degrees (°) North at the North Pole and 90° South at the South Pole. Latitude lines usually have N or S to indicate the Northern or Southern Hemisphere.

Lines of longitude, or meridians, circle the Earth from pole to pole. These lines measure the distance from the Prime Meridian, at 0° longitude. Lines of longitude are not parallel. They usually have an E or a W next to the number to indicate the Eastern or Western Hemisphere.

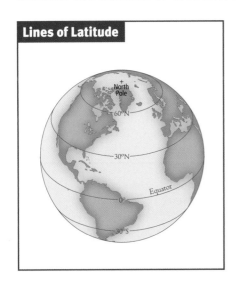

Lines of Latitude

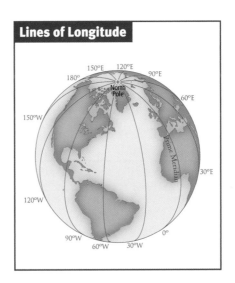

Lines of Longitude

Absolute and Relative Location

You can locate any place on Earth using lines of latitude and longitude. Each line is identified by degrees (°). Each location has a unique number where one line of latitude intersects, or crosses, a line of longitude. This is called its absolute location. Each spot on Earth has an absolute location.

Relative location is the location of a place in relation to other landmarks. For example, St. Louis, Missouri, is located in eastern Missouri, along the Mississippi River.

> **What is your absolute location? Use a map of the United States to find the latitude and longitude of the city or town where you live.**

Maps at Different Scales

All maps are smaller than the real area that they show. To figure out the real distance between two places, most maps include a scale. The scale shows the relationship between distances on a map and real distances.

The scales on the maps in this book are drawn with two horizontal lines. The top line shows distances in miles. The bottom line shows distances in kilometers. You can use a ruler or mark a strip of paper under the scale to measure the distance between places on the map.

The maps on this page are drawn at different scales. Map A and Map B both show the Hawaiian Islands, but Map B shows a larger area with less detail. It is a small-scale map. Map A is a large-scale map. It shows a smaller area with more detail. The scales are different, but the distance between the places shown on both maps is the same.

On both maps, what is the distance in miles between Niihau and Molokai?

What details on Map A are not on Map B?

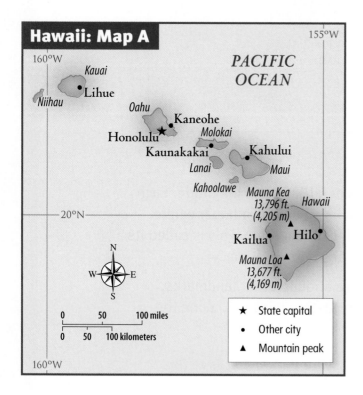

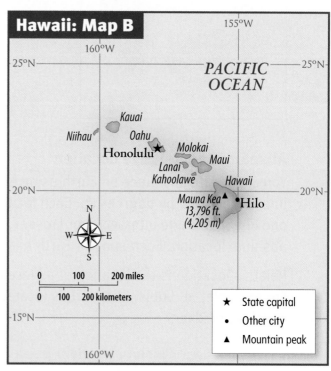

Use Population Maps

When you need to know the number of people who live in a place, or where people live, you can look at a population map. Most population maps show population density—how many people live in a certain area. Another kind of population map shows population distribution—where in an area people live.

Look at the population distribution map of the United States below. Population distribution maps often use different colors to stand for numbers of people per square mile or kilometer. The map key shows the number each color stands for. For example, between 5 and 24 people per square mile live in areas that are shaded yellow.

Which color is used to show the areas with the most people?

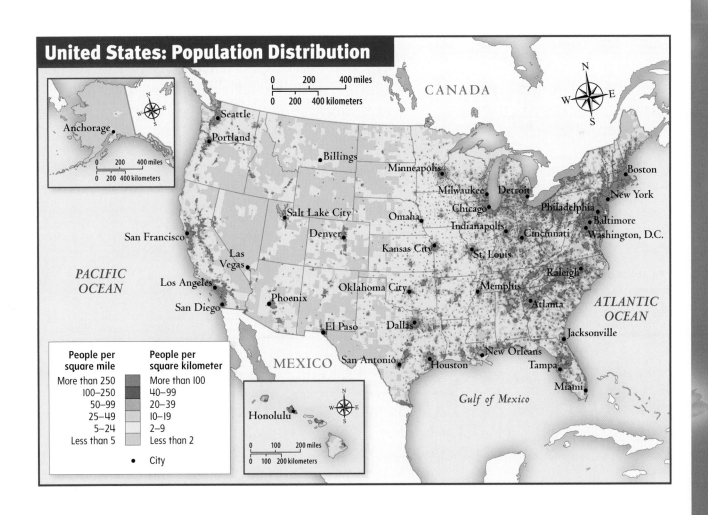

Alaska Inset
ARCTIC OCEAN
70°N

RUSSIA

BROOKS RANGE
ALASKA

CANADA

Arctic Circle

Mt. McKinley
20,320 ft.
(6,194 m)

ALASKA RANGE

Yukon River

Bering Strait

60°N

Bering Sea

Gulf of Alaska

Aleutian Islands

0   200   400 miles
0   200   400 kilometers

170°W   160°W   150°W   140°W   130°W

40°N

Main Map

PACIFIC OCEAN

Puget Sound

Mt. Rainier
14,410 ft. (4,392 m)   WA

Mt. St. Helens
8,363 ft. (2,549 m)

Columbia R.

Mt. Hood
11,239 ft.
(3,426 m)

OR

COLUMBIA PLATEAU

ROCKY

ID

MT

Missouri River

Granite Peak
12,799 ft.
(3,901 m)

Snake River

WY

BLACK HILLS

Mt. Shasta
14,162 ft.
(4,317 m)

CASCADE RANGE

COAST RANGES

Cape Mendocino

Sacramento R.

CENTRAL VALLEY

SIERRA NEVADA

San Joaquin R.

San Francisco Bay

Lake Tahoe

GREAT BASIN

Great Salt Lake

GREAT SALT LAKE DESERT

WASATCH RANGE

Kings Peak
13,528 ft.
(4,123 m)

MOUNTAINS

Mt. Elbert
14,433 ft.
(4,399 m)

CO

NV

UT

COLORADO PLATEAU

Pikes Peak
14,110 ft. (4,30

Mt. Whitney
14,494 ft.
(4,418 m)

CA

Death Valley
-282 ft.
(-86 m)

Lake Mead

Colorado River

Wheeler Peak
13,161 ft.
(4,011 m)

MOJAVE DESERT

Salton Sea

AZ

Humphreys Peak
12,633 ft.
(3,851 m)

CONTINENTAL DIVIDE

Pecos River

Channel Islands

Gila River

SONORAN DESERT

Colorado River

NM

Guadalupe Peak
8,749 ft.
(2,667 m)

Rio Grande

30°N

Legend
Interational boundary
State boundary
⍟ National capital
▲ Mountain peak
▲ Highest point
▼ Lowest point

Hawaii Inset
160°W   155°W

HAWAII

Kauai

Oahu

Niihau

PACIFIC OCEAN

Molokai

Lanai   Maui

Kahoolawe

Hawaii

20°N

Mauna Kea
13,796 ft.
(4,205 m)

0   100   200 miles
0   100   200 kilometers

Scale (main map)
0   200   400 miles
0   200   400 kilometers

Gulf of California

MEXICO

Tropic of Cancer

20°N

120°W   110°W

CANADA

Lake of the Woods

MESABI RANGE

Lake Superior

GREAT LAKES

St. Lawrence River

ME

Mt. Washington 6,288 ft. (1,917 m) ▲

VT

NH

ND

ADIRONDACK MOUNTAINS

GREEN MOUNTAINS

Lake Huron

MN

Lake Ontario

Cape Cod

SD

WI

Lake Michigan

MI

NY

Hudson River

MA

CT RI

Lake Erie

Mississippi River

NE

IA

CENTRAL PLAINS

Long Island

ALLEGHENY PLATEAU

PA

Susquehanna River

NJ

40°N

Platte River

Missouri River

River

OH

ALLEGHENY MOUNTAINS

MD DE

Delaware Bay

IL

IN

Washington, D.C. ⍟

Wabash River

Ohio River

WV

Potomac River

Chesapeake Bay

KS

KY

VA

(1 m)

MO

INTERIOR PLAINS

PIEDMONT

Cape Hatteras

OZARK PLATEAU

Tennessee River

Mt. Mitchell 6,684 ft. (2,037 m) ▲

NC

ATLANTIC COASTAL PLAIN

OK

OUACHITA MOUNTAINS

AR

TN

APPALACHIAN MOUNTAINS

SC

ATLANTIC OCEAN

Red River

Savannah River

Brazos River

AL

Alabama River

GA

Chattahoochee River

TX

MS

30°N

Colorado River

LA

GULF COASTAL PLAIN

EDWARDS PLATEAU

Mobile Bay

FL

Galveston Bay

Mississippi River Delta

Lake Okeechobee

BAHAMAS

Gulf of Mexico

N
W · E
S

CUBA

Florida Keys

Straits of Florida

20°N

50°N

GREAT PLAINS

100°W

90°W

80°W

GH15

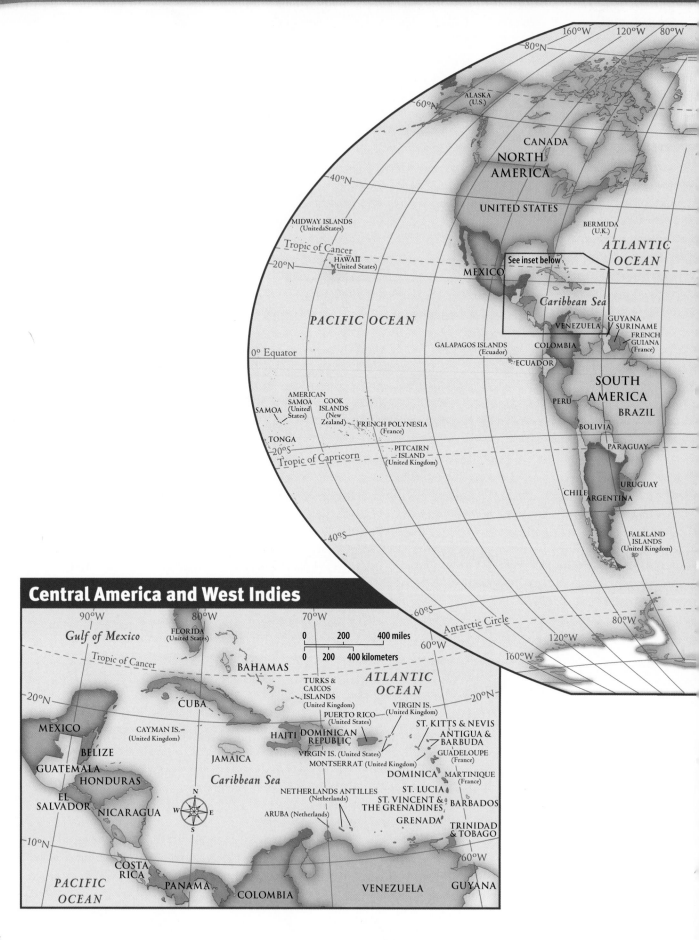

Central America and West Indies

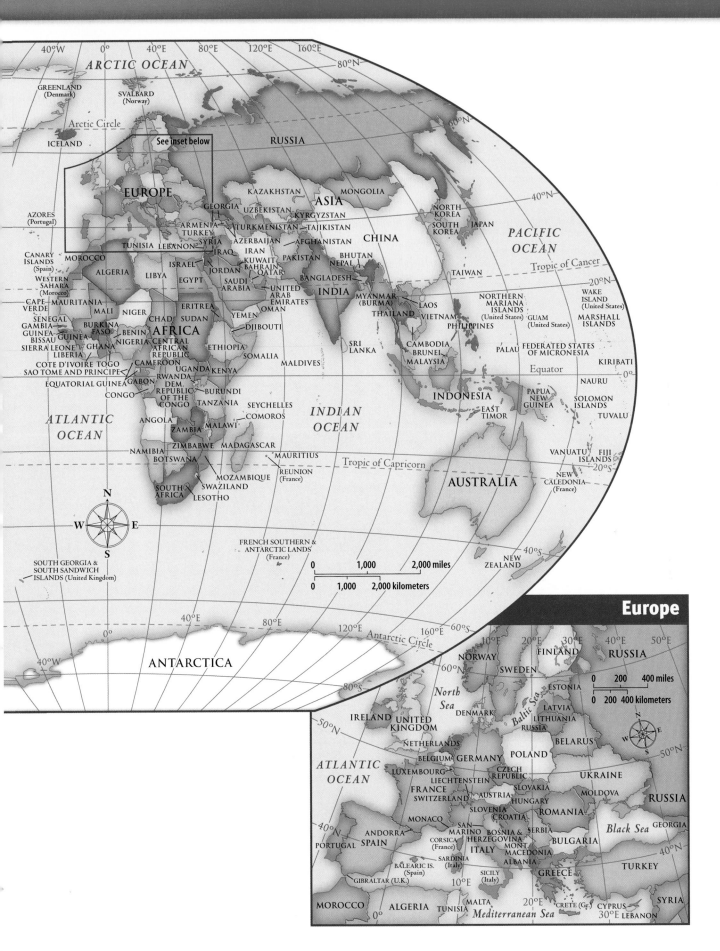

GH17

WI

Zion
Waukegan

Lake Michigan

MI

Freeport   Rockford ✈   Belvidere

Elgin   Des Plaines   Evanston

Sycamore   Wheaton ✈   Chicago ✈

42°N   Dixon   De Kalb

Sterling   Aurora   Naperville

Rock Island   Moline ✈   Joliet

IA   Kewanee   Morris   Ottawa

Streator   Kankakee

Galesburg   Pontiac   N
                                        W   E
                                           S

Peoria ✈   Washington

Canton   Pekin   Normal

Macomb   Bloomington ✈

Lincoln   Champaign   Danville

40°N   Quincy ✈   Urbana ✈

Jacksonville   ★ Springfield ✈   Decatur ✈   IN

Taylorville

Mattoon   Charleston

Effingham

Alton

East
St. Louis ✈   Centralia

Mount Vernon   MO

38°N

Herrin ✈
Carbondale   Marion

	State boundary
✈	Airport
★	State capital
•	Other city

0   25   50 miles
0   25   50 kilometers

92°W

90°W   88°W

GH18

KY

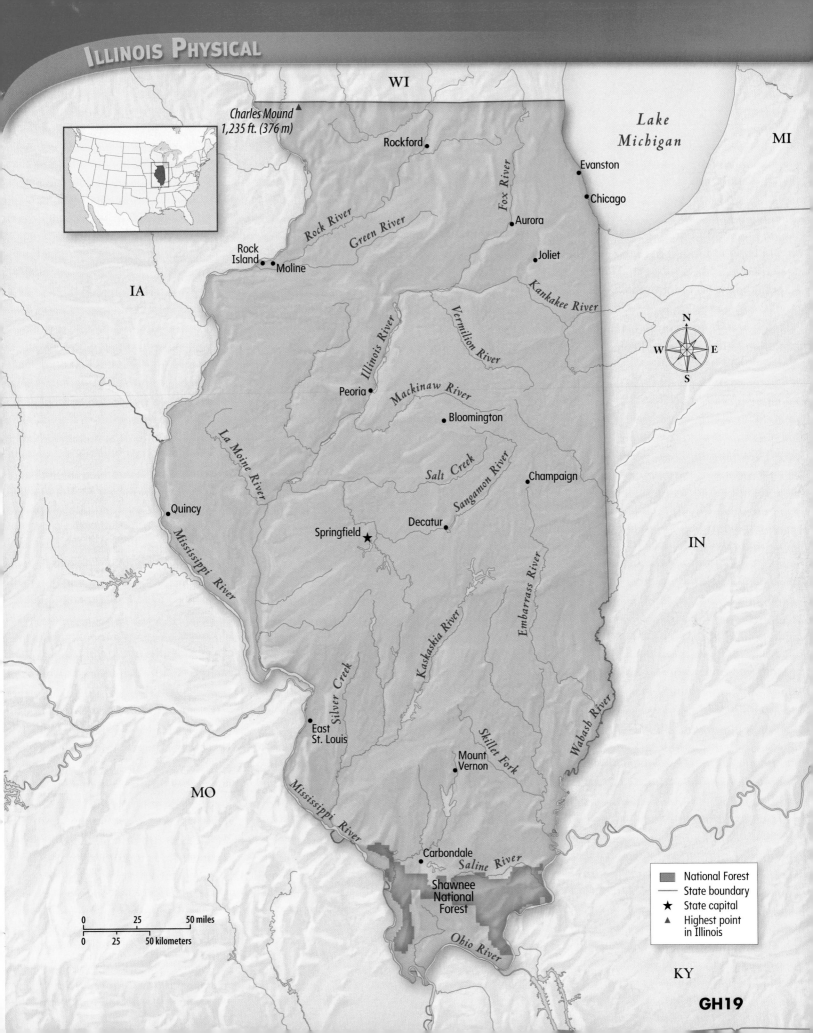

WI

MI

Lake
Michigan

Charles Mound
1,235 ft. (376 m)

Rockford

Evanston

Chicago

Fox River

Rock River

Green River

Aurora

Rock
Island
Moline

Joliet

IA

Kankakee River

Illinois River

Vermilion River

Peoria

Mackinaw River

Bloomington

N

W   E

S

La Moine River

Salt Creek

Sangamon River

Champaign

Quincy

Decatur

Springfield ★

IN

Mississippi River

Embarrass River

Kaskaskia River

Silver Creek

East
St. Louis

Skillet Fork

Mount
Vernon

Wabash River

MO

Mississippi River

Carbondale

Saline River

Shawnee
National
Forest

Ohio River

KY

0   25   50 miles

0   25   50 kilometers

National Forest
State boundary
★ State capital
▲ Highest point
   in Illinois

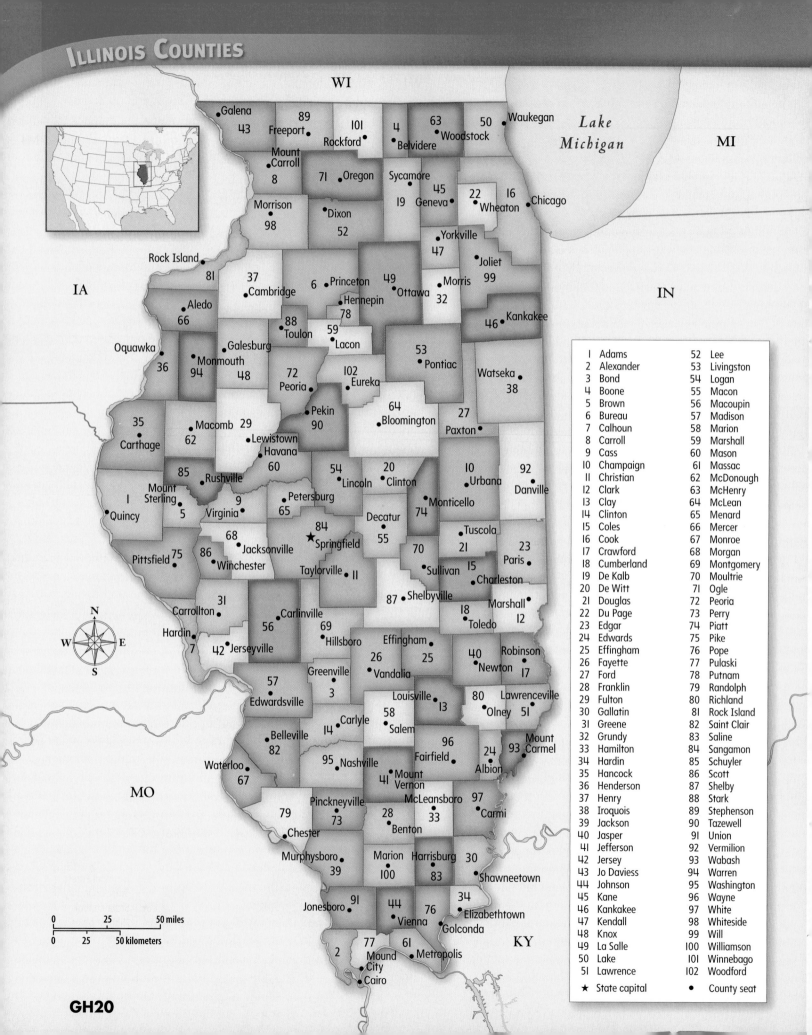

WI

Lake Michigan

MI

IN

IA

MO

KY

• Galena
43
89
Freeport
101
Rockford
4
Belvidere
63
Woodstock
50
Waukegan

Mount Carroll
8
71
Oregon
Sycamore
45
22
Wheaton
16
Chicago

Morrison
98
Dixon
52
19
Geneva
Yorkville
47
Joliet
99

Rock Island
81
37
Cambridge
6
Princeton
49
Ottawa
Morris
32
Kankakee
46

Aledo
66
88
Toulon
Hennepin
78
59
Lacon
53
Pontiac
Watseka
38

Oquawka
36
Monmouth
94
48
Galesburg
72
Peoria
102
Eureka
27
Paxton

35
Carthage
Macomb
62
29
Lewistown
Havana
60
Pekin
90
64
Bloomington

Mount Sterling
85
Rushville
9
Virginia
Petersburg
65
54
Lincoln
20
Clinton
10
Urbana
92
Danville

1
Quincy
5
68
Jacksonville
84
★ Springfield
Decatur
55
74
Monticello
Tuscola
21
23
Paris

Pittsfield
75
86
Winchester
Taylorville
11
70
Sullivan
15
Charleston

31
Carrollton
56
Carlinville
69
87
Shelbyville
18
Toledo
Marshall
12

Hardin
7
42
Jerseyville
Hillsboro
26
Vandalia
Effingham
25
40
Newton
Robinson
17

57
Edwardsville
Greenville
3
Louisville
58
Salem
13
80
Olney
Lawrenceville
51

Waterloo
67
14
Carlyle
95
Nashville
96
Fairfield
24
Albion
93
Mount Carmel

Belleville
82
41
Mount Vernon
McLeansboro
97
Carmi

79
Chester
Pinckneyville
73
28
Benton
33

Murphysboro
39
Marion
100
Harrisburg
83
30
Shawneetown

91
Jonesboro
44
Vienna
76
34
Elizabethtown
Golconda

2
77
Mound City
Cairo
61
Metropolis

N W E S

0   25   50 miles
0   25   50 kilometers

1	Adams	52	Lee
2	Alexander	53	Livingston
3	Bond	54	Logan
4	Boone	55	Macon
5	Brown	56	Macoupin
6	Bureau	57	Madison
7	Calhoun	58	Marion
8	Carroll	59	Marshall
9	Cass	60	Mason
10	Champaign	61	Massac
11	Christian	62	McDonough
12	Clark	63	McHenry
13	Clay	64	McLean
14	Clinton	65	Menard
15	Coles	66	Mercer
16	Cook	67	Monroe
17	Crawford	68	Morgan
18	Cumberland	69	Montgomery
19	De Kalb	70	Moultrie
20	De Witt	71	Ogle
21	Douglas	72	Peoria
22	Du Page	73	Perry
23	Edgar	74	Piatt
24	Edwards	75	Pike
25	Effingham	76	Pope
26	Fayette	77	Pulaski
27	Ford	78	Putnam
28	Franklin	79	Randolph
29	Fulton	80	Richland
30	Gallatin	81	Rock Island
31	Greene	82	Saint Clair
32	Grundy	83	Saline
33	Hamilton	84	Sangamon
34	Hardin	85	Schuyler
35	Hancock	86	Scott
36	Henderson	87	Shelby
37	Henry	88	Stark
38	Iroquois	89	Stephenson
39	Jackson	90	Tazewell
40	Jasper	91	Union
41	Jefferson	92	Vermilion
42	Jersey	93	Wabash
43	Jo Daviess	94	Warren
44	Johnson	95	Washington
45	Kane	96	Wayne
46	Kankakee	97	White
47	Kendall	98	Whiteside
48	Knox	99	Will
49	La Salle	100	Williamson
50	Lake	101	Winnebago
51	Lawrence	102	Woodford
★	State capital	•	County seat

Glossary

This Glossary will help you to pronounce and understand the meanings of the vocabulary terms in this book. The page number at the end of the definition tells you where the word first appears.

PRONUNCIATION KEY

a	at	ē	me	ō	old	ū	use	ng	song
ā	ape	i	it	ô	fork	ü	rule	th	thin
ä	far	ī	ice	oi	oil	ù	pull	th	this
âr	care	î	pierce	ou	out	ûr	turn	zh	measure
e	end	o	hot	u	up	hw	white	ə	about, taken, pencil, lemon, circus

A

A.D. (ā dē) "Anno Domini." Latin for "in the year of the Lord." Used before a numeral to indicate a year occurring since the birth of Jesus Christ (p. 27)

abolitionist (ab ə lish'ə nist) a person who wanted to end slavery in the United States (p. 251)

absolute location (ab sə lüt' lō kā'shən) the exact location of a place expressed by longitude and latitude or street address (p. 59)

Adams-Onís Treaty (ad' əmz ō'nēs' trē'tē) Spain's agreement to sell Florida to the United States (p. 219)

adobe (a dō'bē) a type of clay traditionally used as a building material by Native Americans and, later, Spanish colonists in the Southwest (p. 24)

ally (a'lī) a person, group, or nation united with another in order to do something (p. 83)

amendment (ə mend'mənt) an addition to the Constitution. See **Constitution**. (p. 209)

ammunition (am ū nish'ən) objects, such as bullets, that can be fired from a weapon (p. 163)

Anaconda Plan (an ə kon'da plan) the Union's three-part plan for defeating the Confederacy and ending the Civil War (p. 262)

annex (ə neks') to make a country or territory part of another country (p. 313)

apprentice (ə pren' tis) a person learning a craft or trade from a master (p. 120)

archaeologists (är kē ol'ə jist) a scientist who looks for and studies artifacts. See **artifact** (p. 21)

arms race (ärmz rās) the effort build and acquire the most powerful weapons (p. 349)

arsenal (ar 'sə nəl) a storage place for weapons (p. 198)

Articles of Confederation (är'ti kalz uv kən fed ə rā'shən) the first plan of government of the United States. It gave more power to the states than to the central government. See **Constitution** (p. 197)

artifact (är'ti fakt) an object made by humans long ago (p. 12)

assassination (ə sas ə nā 'shən) the murder of an important person (p. 278)

assembly (ə sem'blē) a lawmaking body (p. 137)

assembly line (ə sem' blē līn) a method of mass production in which the product is carried on a moving belt past workers (p.335)

B

B.C. (bē sē) Before Christ. Used after a numeral to indicate a year occurring before the birth of Jesus Christ (p. 27)

B.C.E. (bē sē ē) Before the Common Era. See **B.C.** (p. 27)

backcountry (bak kun'trē) Colonial area between the Appalachian Mountains and the Atlantic Coastal Plain (p. 122)

barter (bär' tər) the trading of goods for goods (p. 54)

battle map (bat'əl map) a map that shows the events of a conflict between two groups of armed forces (p. 177)

bill of rights (bil əv rīts) a formal statement of rights and liberties guaranteed to the people by a state. See **amendment** and **constitution** (p. 209)

black codes (blak kōdz) laws passed by the Southern states after the Civil War that severely limited the rights of the newly freed African Americans (p. 281)

blockade (blok ād') a barrier preventing the movement of troops and supplies (p. 187)

boycott (boi'kot) to refuse to do business or have contact with a person, group, company, country, or product (p. 157)

buffalo soldier (bəf ə 'lō sōl djər) an African-American soldier serving in the western United States after the Civil War (p. 314)

C

C.E. (sē ē) "Common Era" (p. 27)

campaign (kam pān') a series of military operations intended to achieve an important goal in war (p. 379)

cartogram (kär'tə gram) a map that shows information by changing the sizes of places (p. 311)

cash crop (kash krop) a crop that is grown to be sold for profit (p. 88)

cattle drive (kat' əl drīv) the movement of large herds of cattle, by cowboys, from ranches to the railroad (p. 293)

census (sen'səs) an official count of all the people living in a country or region (p. 6)

century (sen'chə rē) a period of 100 years (p. 27)

charter (chär'tər) an official document giving a person permission to do something, such as settle in an area (p. 87)

circa (sûr'kə) in approximately (p. 27)

circle graph (sûr'kəl graf) a kind of chart that shows how something can be divided into parts (p. 77)

citizen (sit'ə zən) A person born in a country or who legally becomes a member of that country (p. 9)

PRONUNCIATION KEY

a	at	ē	me	ō	old	ū	use	ng	song
ā	ape	i	it	ô	fork	ü	rule	th	thin
ä	far	ī	ice	oi	oil	u̇	pull	th	this
âr	care	î	pierce	ou	out	ûr	turn	zh	measure
e	end	o	hot	u	up	hw	white	ə	about, taken, pencil, lemon, circus

Civil Rights Act (siv'el rīts akt) a law that guarantees the individual rights of all citizens to be treated equally under the law (p. 354)

civil war (siv'əl wôr) an armed conflict between groups within one country. In the United States, the war between the Union and the Confederacy from 1861 to 1865 (p.257)

civilization (siv ə lə zā'shən) A culture that has developed complex systems of government, education, and religion. Civilizations usually have large populations with many people living in cities (p. 22)

clan (klan) a group of families who share the same ancestor (p. 44)

climate (klī'mit) the weather of an area over a number of years (pp. 4, 249)

climograph (klī'mō graf) a graph that shows information about the temperature and precipitation of a place over time (p. 249)

colony (kol'ə nē) a settlement far away from the country that rules it (p. 63)

Columbian Exchange (kə lum'bē ən eks chānj') the movement of people, plants, animals, and germs in either direction across the Atlantic Ocean following the voyages of Columbus (p. 64)

commerce (kom'ərs) the buying and selling of goods (p. 380)

commodity (kə mod'i tē) basic goods that are bought and sold (p. 396)

common (kom'ən) the village green or center of Puritan villages characterized by the presence of a Puritan church or meeting house (p. 102)

communism (kom'ū nism) the political system in which the government owns all property and distributes resources to its citizens (p. 347)

commute (kə 'myüt) to travel back and forth regularly (p. 307)

concentration camps (kon sen trā shun kamps) prisons where Nazis enslaved and murdered millions of people during WW II (p. 345)

conductor (kən duk'tər) a person who helped enslaved people escaping on the Underground Railroad reach freedom (p. 387)

conquistador (kon kēs'tə dôr) a name for the Spanish conquerors who first came to the Americas in the 1500s (p. 67)

Continental army (kon'tə nen'təl är'mē) the army created by the Second Continental Congress in May 1775 with George Washington as commander-in-chief (p. 149)

corporation (kôr pə rā'shən) a form of business in which holders of shares of stock are the owners of the business (p. 304)

cost-benefit decision (kost 'ben ə fit dis izh'ən) A choice made to buy a product taking into consideration the future benefits that will result from the product (p. 11)

cotton gin (kot'ən jin) a machine that separates cotton from its seeds, invented by Eli Whitney in 1793 (p. 223)

coup stick (kü stik) a weapon used by a Lakota Sioux fighter to show bravery by touching, but not killing, an enemy (p. 39)

coureurs de bois (kü rər' də bwä') in New France, a person who trapped furs without permission from the French government (p. 84)

covenant (ku' və nənt) a contract, an agreement (p. 102)

Creek Confederacy (krēk kən fed'ər ə sē) the union formed by several groups of Creek Indians to protect themselves (p. 44)

culture (kul'chər) the entire way of life of a people, including their customs, beliefs, and language (p. 12)

D

debate (dē bāt') a formal argument about different political ideas (p. 255)

debtor (det'ər) a person who owes money (p. 115)

Declaration of Independence (dek lə rā'shən əv in də pen'dəns) the official document issued on July 4, 1776, announcing that the American colonies were breaking away from Great Britain (p. 150)

deforestation (dē fôr'ist ā'shən) the cutting down of large numbers of trees (p. 375)

delegate (del'ə git) a member of an elected assembly. See **assembly** (p.159)

demand (di mand') the desire for a product or service. See **supply** (p. 11)

desert (di'zərt) to go away and leave a person or thing that should not be left (p.179)

dictator (dik'tā tor) ruler or leader with absolute power (p. 341)

discrimination (di skrim ə nā'shən) an unfair difference in the treatment of people (p. 231)

draft (draft) the selecting of persons for military service or some other special duty (p. 259)

E

economy (i kon'ə mē) the way a country's people use natural resources, money, and knowledge to produce goods and services (p. 10)

ecosystem (ē'kō sis'təm) all the living and nonliving things in a certain area (p. 3)

Emancipation Proclamation (ē man si pā'shən prok lə mā'shən) the official announcement issued by President Abraham Lincoln in 1862 that led to the end of slavery in the United States (p. 267)

empire (em'pīr) an area in which different groups of people are controlled by one ruler or government (p. 67)

enslave (en slāv') to force a person to work for no money without the freedom to leave (p.75)

environment (en vī'rən mənt) all the surroundings in which people, plants, and animals live (p. 3)

Era of Good Feelings (îr'ə uv gůd fē'lingz) the name given to the period of peace and prosperity that followed the War of 1812 (p. 219)

era (îr'ə) a period of time or history (p. 351)

ethnic group (eth'nik grüp) people who share the same customs and language, and often a common history (p. 7)

exoduster (ek'so dus tər) An African American from the South who went to Kansas in the 1870s (p. 297)

expedition (ek spi dish'ən) a journey made for a special purpose (p. 61)

export (ek'spôrt) to send goods to other countries for sale or use (p. 84)

F

federal system (fed'ər əl sis'təm) a system of government in which power in the nation is shared between the central government and the state governments (p. 205)

free state (frē stāt) state where slavery was banned (p. 246)

French and Indian War (french ənd in'dē ən wôr) a conflict between Great Britain and France in North America from 1756 to 1763 (p. 153)

frontier (frun tēr') the name given by colonists to the far end of a country where people are just beginning to settle (p. 73)

PRONUNCIATION KEY

a	at	ē	me	ō	old	ū	use	ng	song
ā	ape	i	it	ô	fork	ü	rule	th	thin
ä	far	ī	ice	oi	oil	ù	pull	th	this
âr	care	î	pierce	ou	out	ûr	turn	zh	measure
e	end	o	hot	u	up	hw	white	ə	about, taken, pencil, lemon, circus

fundamental (fun də men'təl) something basic or necessary (p. 103)

G

Gettysburg Address (get'iz burg ə dres') a speech made by President Lincoln at the site of the Battle of Gettysburg in 1863 (p. 271)

glacier (glā' shər) a large mass of ice (p. 21)

global grid (glō'bəl grid) a set of squares formed by crisscrossing lines that can help you determine the absolute location of a place on a globe (p. 59)

global warming (glō' bəl wär' ming) the gradual increase of the Earth's temperature (p. 364)

Gold Rush (gōld rush) the sudden rush of people to an area where gold has been discovered (p. 236)

Great Awakening (grāt ə wā' kən ing) a religious movement of the 1700s (p. 121)

gross state product (grōs stāt prod'ukt) total value of goods and services produced within the state in a year (p. 396)

growth rate (grōth rāt) an increase or decrease of something expressed in percentage (p. 121)

H

historian (hi stōr'ē ən) a person who studies the past (p. 12)

historical map (his tôr'i kəl map) a map that shows information about the past or where past events took place (p.123)

hogan (hō'gən) a Navajo dwelling (p. 35)

homesteader (hōm' sted ər) a person who claimed land on the Great Plains under the Homestead Act of 1862 (p. 295)

House of Burgesses (hous uv bər'jis əz) the law-making body of colonial Virginia, established in Jamestown in 1619 (p. 89)

I

immigrant (im'ə grənt) a person who leaves one country to live in another (p. 6)

import (im'pōrt) to bring goods from another country for sale or use (p. 84)

impressment (im pres ' mənt) the act of seizing for public use or service (p. 215)

indentured servant (in den'chərd sûr'vənt) a person who worked for someone in colonial America for a set time in exchange for the ocean voyage (p. 89)

indigo (in'di gō) a plant that is used to produce a blue dye. See **cash crop** (p. 114)

Industrial Revolution (in dəs'trē əl rev ə lü'shən) the change from making goods by hand at home to making them by machine in factories (p. 223)

industry (in' dəs trē) a branch of business, trade, or manufacturing (p. 134)

inflation (in flā' shən) a rise in the usual price of goods and services (p. 176)

interchangeable part (in tər chan'jə bəl part) parts of a product built to a standard size so that they can be easily replaced (p. 223)

interdependence (in'tər di pen'dəns) dependence on each other to meet needs and wants (p. 364)

internment (in tərn' ment) the isolation and confinement of people during a war (p. 343)

Iroquois Confederacy (îr'ə kwä kən fed'ər ə sē) the union of the five major Iroquois peoples beginning about 1570 (p. 45)

irrigation (ir i gā'shən) a method of supplying dry land with water though a series of ditches or pipes (p. 24)

J

Jim Crow laws (jim krō lôz) laws passed by Southern states after Reconstruction that established segregation, or separation of the races. See **segregation** (p. 285)

L

labor union (lā'bər ūn'yən) a group of workers united to gain better wages and working conditions (p.305)

large-scale map (lärj skāl map) a map that shows a smaller area in greater detail (p. 177)

latitude (lat'i tüd) an imaginary line, or parallel, measuring distance north or south of the equator. See **parallel** (p. 59)

League of Nations (lēg əv nā'shuns) an organization formed in 1920 by the Allied Powers of WW I to prevent further wars (p. 330)

legislation (le jəs lā'shən) laws passed by a law-making body (p. 137)

legislature (lej'is lā' chər) a body of people that has the power to make or pass laws (p. 200)

line graph (līn graf) a kind of graph that shows changes over time (p. 77)

lodge (loj) a type of home made of logs, grasses, sticks, and soil, which Native Americans of the Plains used when living in their villages. See **teepee** (p. 37)

longhouse (lông'hous) a home shared by several related Iroquois families (p. 43)

longitude (lon'ji tüd) an imaginary line, or meridian, measuring distance east or west of the prime meridian. See **meridian** and **prime meridian** (p. 59)

loyalist (loi'ə list) a colonist who supported Great Britain in the American Revolution (p. 172)

M

malice (ma' ləs) to want to harm someone (p. 278)

manifest destiny (man'ə fest des'tə nē) belief in the early 1800s that the United States was to stretch west to the Pacific Ocean and south to the Rio Grande (p. 229)

map scale (map skāl) a line drawn on a map that uses a unit of measurement, such as an inch, to represent a real distance on Earth (p. 221)

mass production (mas prō duk' shun) making large quantities of an item in order to keep costs low (p. 335)

mercenary (mûr'sə nər ē) a soldier paid to fight for another country (p. 172)

merchant (mûr'chənt) a person who buys, sells, and trades goods for a profit (p. 54)

merchant company (mûr'chənt kum'pə nē) a group of merchants who share the cost and profits of a business (p. 80)

meridian (mə rid'ē ən) any line of longitude east or west of Earth's prime meridian. See **longitude** and **prime meridian** (p. 59)

mestizo (me stē'zō) a person of mixed Spanish and Indian heritage (p. 76)

PRONUNCIATION KEY

a	at	ē	me	ō	old	ū	use	ng	song
ā	ape	i	it	ô	fork	ü	rule	th	thin
ä	far	ī	ice	oi	oil	ů	pull	th	this
âr	care	î	pierce	ou	out	ûr	turn	zh	measure
e	end	o	hot	u	up	hw	white	ə	about, taken, pencil, lemon, circus

Middle Passage (mid'əl pas'ij) the middle leg of the colonial trade route in which captive Africans were shipped to the West Indies. See **slave trade** and **triangular trade** (p. 133)

migrant farm worker (mī'grənt färm wûr'kər) a laborer who moves from one farm to another as the seasons change (p. 356)

migrate (mī'grāt) to move from one place to another (p. 34)

military draft (mil'i ter' ē draft)) a system that requires people to serve in the armed forces (p. 386)

militia (mə lish'ə) a group of volunteers who fought in times of emergency during the colonial period and the American Revolution (p. 161)

missionary (mish'ə ner ē) a person who teaches his or her religion to those who have different beliefs (p. 75)

Missouri Compromise (mə zûr'ē kom'prə mīz) an agreement in 1820 that allowed Missouri and Maine to enter the Union and divided the Louisiana Territory into areas allowing slavery and areas outlawing slavery (p. 246)

monopoly (mə nop'ə lē) a company that controls an entire industry (p. 304)

Monroe Doctrine (mən rō dok'trin) a declaration of United States foreign policy made by President James Monroe in 1823 that opposed European colonization or interference in the Western Hemisphere (p. 220)

muckraker (muk rā'kər) a newspaper writer who points out the misbehavior of public figures (p. 325)

N

navigation (nav ə gā'shən) the science of determining a ship's location and direction (p. 57)

neutral (nü'trəl) not taking sides (p. 341)

nomad (nō'mad) a person who wanders from place to place (p. 373)

North American Free Trade Agreement (nôrth ə mer'i kən frē trād ə grē'mənt) a treaty signed by the United States, Canada, and Mexico in 1992 that makes all of North America one trading area (p. 364)

Northwest Passage (nôrth'west pas'ij) a water route believed to flow through North America to Asia that European explorers searched for from the 1500s to the 1700s (p. 79)

Northwest Territory (nôrth'west' ter'i tôr'ē) an area of land between the Great Lakes and the Ohio River, established in 1787 (p. 380)

O

opportunity cost (äp ôr tün'ə tē kost) the value of the second best choice when choosing between two things (p. 11)

P

parallel (par'ə lel) a line of latitude. See **latitude** (p. 59)

parallel time line (par'ə lel tīm'līn) two different sets of events on the same time line (p. 27)

Patriot (pā'trē ət) an American colonist who supported the fight for independence (p. 171)

patroon (pə trün') the name given to wealthy Dutch landowners who were given land to farm along the Hudson River by the Dutch West India Company in the 1600s (p. 107)

pilgrim (pil' grəm) a person who travels to a place for religious reasons (p. 90)

pioneer (pī ə nîr') a person who is among the first of nonnative people to settle a region (p. 213)

plantation (plan tā'shən) a large farm that often grows one cash crop (p. 114)

political map (pə lit'i kəl map) a map that illustrates divisions between territories such as nations, states, or other political units (p. 397)

potlatch (pot'lach) a feast given by Native Americans of the northwest coast, in which the guests receive gifts (p. 31)

poverty (päv'ər tē) the condition of being poor (p. 297)

prejudice (pre'jə dis) a negative opinion formed beforehand or without proof (p. 355)

primary source (prī'mer ē sôrs) a firsthand account of an event or an artifact created during the period of history that is being studied. See **artifact** and **secondary source** (p. 12)

prime meridian (prīm mə rid'ē ən) the line of longitude labeled 0° longitude. Any place east of the prime meridian is labeled E. Any place west of it is labeled W. See **longitude** (p. 59)

Proclamation of 1763 (prok lə mā'shən) an official announcement by King George III of Great Britain that outlawed colonial settlement west of the Appalachian Mountains (p. 154)

profit (prof' it) the money made on goods that exceeds the cost of production. (p. 54)

profiteering (prof'it ēr ing) making excess profits from goods that are in short supply (p. 176)

progressive (prə gres'iv) making use of new and creative ideas for change (p. 325)

property rights (prä'pər tē rīts) the rights to own or use something (p. 299)

proprietor (prə prī'ə tər) a person who owns property or a business (p. 108)

proslavery (prō slā'və rē) supporting slavery (p. 381)

ratify (rat'ə fi) to officially approve (p. 208)

ration (ra'shən) to control the distribution of supplies (p. 342)

reaper (rē'pər) a machine that cuts grain for harvesting (p. 224)

Reconstruction (rē kən struk'shən) the rebuilding of the South after the Civil War (p. 281)

reform (ri fôrm') a change to improve the lives of many people (p. 325)

region (rē'jən) a large area with common features that set it apart from other areas (p. 4)

relative location (rel ə tiv lō kā'shən) a place in relation to another (p. 59)

repeal (ri pēl') to cancel (p. 157)

reservation (re sər vā'shun) territories set aside for Native Americans (p. 299)

S

sachem (sā'chəm) an Iroquois chief or tribal leader (p. 92)

satellite (sat'ə līt) an object that circles a larger object such as a moon (p. 350)

secede (si sēd') to withdraw from the Union (p. 257)

PRONUNCIATION KEY

a	at	ē	me	ō	old	ū	use	ng	song
ā	ape	i	it	ô	fork	ü	rule	th	thin
ä	far	ī	ice	oi	oil	ù	pull	th	this
âr	care	î	pierce	ou	out	ûr	turn	zh	measure
e	end	o	hot	u	up	hw	white	ə	about, taken, pencil, lemon, circus

secondary source (sek'ən der ē sôrs) an account of the past based on information from primary sources and written by someone who was not an eyewitness to those events. See **primary source** (p. 12)

segregation (seg ri gā'shən) separation of people based on race (p. 285)

settlement house (set'əl mənt hous) institutions located in poor neighborhoods that provided numerous community services (p. 391)

sharecropping (shâr'krop ing) a system in which farmers rented land in return for crops (p. 282)

slash-and-burn (slash and bûrn) to cut and burn trees to clear land for farming (p. 41)

slave codes (slāv cōdz) rules made by colonial planters that controlled the lives of enslaved Africans (p. 125)

slave state (slāv stāt) state where slavery was allowed (p. 246)

slave trade (slāv trād) the business of buying and selling people (p. 119)

slavery (slā'və rē) the practice of treating people as property and forcing them to work (p. 104)

slum (slum) a rundown neighborhood (p. 308)

small-scale map (smôl skāl map) a map that shows a large area but not much detail. (p. 221)

Spanish-American War (span'ish ə mer'ikən wôr) the war between the United States and Spain in 1898 in which the United States gained control of Puerto Rico, Guam, and the Philippines (p. 315)

spiritual (spi' ri tū əl) the religious songs of enslaved Africans (p. 127)

Stamp Act (stamp akt) a law passed by the British requiring colonists to pay a tax on paper products (p. 157)

station (stā'shən) a regular stopping place along a route (p. 386)

steam engine (stēm en'jin) an engine that is powered by compressed steam (p. 224)

stock (stok) a share in the ownership of a company (p. 337)

strike (strīk) a refusal of all the workers in a business to work until the owners meet their demands (p. 305)

suffrage (suf'rij) the right to vote (p. 333)

supply (sə plī') a quantity of something needed or ready for use. See **demand** (p. 11)

supply depot (sə plī' dē'pō) where military supplies are stored (p. 386)

Supreme Court (sü prēm' kôrt) the head of the judicial branch of the federal government. It is the highest court in the country (p. 205)

sweatshop (swet'shop) shops or factories where employees worked long hours under poor conditions for low wages (p. 391)

T

tariff (tar' ef) a tax placed on imports or exports to control the sale price (p. 247)

technological (tek'nə loj'i kəl) scientific knowledge that can solve practical problems (p. 394)

tepee (tē'pē) a cone-shaped tent made from animal hides and wooden poles used by Native Americans of the Plains (p. 37)

tenement (ten'ə mənt) rundown building (p. 308)

territory (ter'i tôr ē) an area of land controlled by a nation (p. 149)

terrorism (ter'ər izm) the use of fear and violence by non-government groups against civilians to achieve political goals (p. 361)

time line (tīm' līn) a diagram showing the order in which events took place (p. 27)

time zone (tīm zōn) one of the 24 areas into which Earth is divided for measuring time (p. 331)

tolerate (tol'ə rāt) to allow people to have different beliefs from your own (p. 103)

total war (to' təl wôr) attacking an enemy's soldiers, civilians, and property (p. 264)

totem pole (tō təm pōl) a tree trunk that is carved with sacred images by Native Americans (p. 30)

Trail of Tears (trāl uv tîrz) the name given to the 800-mile forced march of 15,000 Cherokee in 1838 from their homes in Georgia to the Indian Territory (p. 229)

transcontinental railroad (trans kon ti nen'təl rāl'rōd) a railroad that crosses a continent (p. 294)

travois (trə voi') a kind of sled that is dragged to move supplies (p. 38)

treason (trē'zən) the act of betraying one's country (p. 256)

Treaty of Alliance (trē'tē əv ə lī'əns) the treaty signed between France and the United States during the American Revolution (p. 181)

Treaty of Guadalupe Hidalgo (trē'tē uv gwäd ə lü'pā ēdäl'gō) the treaty under which Mexico sold territory to the United States (p. 235)

Treaty of Paris 1763 (trē'tē uv par'əs) the agreement signed by Great Britain and France that brought an end to the French and Indian War (p. 154)

Treaty of Paris 1783 (trē'tē uv par'əs) The peace agreement in which Great Britain recognized the United States as an independent country (p. 187)

Treaty of Versailles (trē'tē əv vər sī') the agreement that ended World War I (p. 330)

triangular trade (trī ang'gyə lər trād) three-sided trade routes over the Atlantic Ocean (p. 132)

tributary (trib' yə ter ē) a river or stream that flows into a larger river (p. 149)

trinket (tring'kit) small, inexpensive ornaments (p. 18)

truce (trüs) an agreement to stop fighting that does not end a war (p. 349)

U

Union (yün'yən) states that are joined together as one political group (p. 277)

V

Voting Rights Act (vō'ting rīts akt) a 1965 law that guarantees U.S. citizens the right to vote (p. 355)

voyageur (vwä yä zhûr') a trader who transported furs by canoe in New France (p. 84)

W

wagon train (wag' ən trān) a group of covered wagons that follow one another closely to a destination (p. 229)

wampum (wom'pəm) polished beads made from shells strung or woven together used in gift-giving and trading by Native Americans (p. 43)

War Hawks (wôr hôks) members of Congress from the South and the West in the early 1800s who wanted the United States to go to war against Great Britain. See **War of 1812** (p. 217)

PRONUNCIATION KEY

a	at	ē	me	ō	old	ū	use	ng	song	
ā	ape	i	it	ô	fork	ü	rule	th	thin	
ä	far	ī	ice	oi	oil	ú	pull	th	this	
âr	care	î	pierce	ou	out	ûr	turn	zh	measure	
e	end	o	hot	u	up	hw	white	ə	about, taken, pencil, lemon, circus	

Index

*This index lists many topics that appear in the book, along with the pages on which they are found. Page numbers after a *c* refer you to a chart or diagram, after a *g*, to a graph, after an *m*, to a map, after a *p*, to a photograph or picture, and after a *q*, to a quotation.

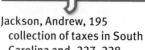

Index

Credits

Musées Nationaux/Art Resource, NY. 148: (bl) Culver Pictures/Art Archive; (br) The Granger Collection, New York. 149: Culver Pictures/Art Archive. 151: The Granger Collection, New York. 152: (bl) The Granger Collection, New York; (br) General Wolfe Museum Quebec House/Eileen Tweedy/Art Archive. 152-153: Artist Robert Griffing and his Publisher Paramount Press Inc. 153: The Granger Collection, New York. 154-155: (bg) General Wolfe Museum Quebec House/Eileen Tweedy/Art Archive. 155: (cl) SuperStock; (cr) The Granger Collection, New York. 156: (bl) Library of Congress, Prints & Photographs Division, [LC-USZC4-1583]; (br) North Wind Picture Archives. 156-157: Library of Congress, Prints & Photographs Division, [LC-USZC4-1583]. 157: The Granger Collection, New York. 158: North Wind Picture Archives. 159: (b) Culver Pictures/Art Archive; (t) Library of Congress, Prints & Photographs Division, [LC-USZC4-1583]. 160: (bc) The Granger Collection, New York; (bl) Bettmann/CORBIS; (br) Phil E. Degginger/Mira. com. 160-161: Bettmann/CORBIS. 162-163: The Granger Collection, New York. 164: SuperStock. 165: (c) Bettmann/CORBIS; (t) Phil E. Degginger/Mira.com. 166: (bl) NTPL/Christopher Hurst/The Image Works, Inc.; (br) Bettmann/CORBIS. 166-167: SuperStock. 167: NTPL/Christopher Hurst/The Image Works, Inc. 168: Bettmann/CORBIS. 169: (c) SuperStock; (t) EPA/Tom Mihalek/Landov. 170: (bcl) Painting by Don Troiani/Historical Art Prints; (bcr) SuperStock; (bl) Painting by Don Troiani/Historical Art Prints; (br) The Granger Collection, New York. 170-171: Painting by Don Troiani/Historical Art Prints. 171: Painting by Don Troiani/Historical Art Prints. 172: (l) Painting by Don Troiani/Historical Art Prints; (r) Painting by Don Troiani/Historical Art Prints. 172-173: (bg) Fine Art Photographic Library/CORBIS. 173: (l) From the original painting by Mort Kunstler, Reading the Declaration of Independence to the Troops. © 1975 Mort Kunstler, Inc. www.

mkunstler.com; (r) Painting by Don Troiani/Historical Art Prints. 174: (bg) Massachusetts Historical Society; (l) SuperStock; (r) The Granger Collection, New York. 175: David Wagner. 176: (c) Painting by Don Troiani/Historical Art Prints; (t) The Granger Collection, New York. 178: (bc) Peter Bowden; (bl) Library of Congress, Prints & Photographs Division, [LC-USZCN4-159]; (br) SuperStock. 179: (l) The Granger Collection, New York; (r) Library of Congress, Prints & Photographs Division, [LC-USZCN4-159]. 180: Flying Fish Photography. 181: (b) Independence National Historical Park; (tl) Kathy McLaughlin/The Image Works, Inc.; (tr) Peter Bowden. 182-183: (b) SuperStock. 184: (bc) SuperStock; (bl) The Granger Collection, New York; (br) Cynthia Hart Designer/CORBIS. 184-185: Michelle & Tom Grimm/Buddy Mays/Travel Stock Photography. 185: The Granger Collection, New York. 186: SuperStock. 187: Erich Lessing/Art Resource, NY. 188-189: (t) Cynthia Hart Designer/CORBIS. 189: (c) Michelle & Tom Grimm/ Buddy Mays/Travel Stock Photography. 190: (b) Victoria & Albert Museum, London/Art Resource, NY; (t) Painting by Don Troiani/Historical Art Prints. 192: (b) The Granger Collection, New York; (t) Dave Mager/Index Stock Imagery.

ACKNOWLEDGMENTS

Grateful acknowledgment is given to the following authors and publishers. Every effort has been made to trace the ownership of all copyrighted material and to secure the necessary permissions to reprint these selections. In the case of some selections for which acknowledgment is not given, extensive research has failed to locate the copyright holders.